D1029360

ETHNOMUSICOLOGY RESEARCH

GARLAND LIBRARY OF
MUSIC ETHNOLOGY
(VOL. 1)

GARLAND REFERENCE LIBRARY
OF THE HUMANITIES
(VOL. 1136)

Garland Library of Music Ethnology
Series Editor: James Porter

1. Ethnomusicology Research: A Select Annotated
   Bibliography
   by Ann Briegleb Schuursma

ETHNOMUSICOLOGY RESEARCH
A Select Annotated Bibliography

Ann Briegleb Schuursma

GARLAND PUBLISHING, INC. • NEW YORK & LONDON
1992

Library of Congress Cataloging-in-Publication Data

Schuursma, Ann Briegleb, 1934–
    Ethnomusicology research : a select annotated bibliography / Ann
Briegleb Schuursma.
        p. cm. — (Garland library of music ethnology ; 1) (Garland
reference library of the humanities ; 1136)
    Includes indexes.
    ISBN 0-8240-5735-X (alk. paper)
    1. Ethnomusicology—Bibliography. I. Title. II. Series.
III. Series: Garland reference library of the humanities ; vol.
1136.
    ML128.E8S4   1992
780'.89—dc20   90-3736
                                             CIP
                                           MN

Printed on acid-free, 250-year-life paper
Manufactured in the United States of America

CONTENTS

SERIES EDITOR'S PREFACE

The Garland Library of Music Ethnology comprises mainly reference works in ethnomusicology, dance ethnology, music anthropology, and related fields. The series seeks to fill some gaps in reference and research: in specific music areas such as Native American, Arab, Southeast Asian, Latin American, European, and North American, and through works of a more general methodological kind. Further contributions to the series will be in dance ethnology, discography, and filmography. In addition, some important works in translation, as well as the occasional monograph, will form part of the series.

The term "music ethnology" was chosen for a practical reason: to differentiate the series from *The Garland Library of Readings in Ethnomusicology* (7 vols., 1990). There are less obvious reasons for using "music ethnology": "ethnomusicology," though it has flourished in scholarly circles since its invention by Jaap Kunst in 1950, is a cumbersome term for the lay person; a certain ambiguity is built into it through the ethno- prefix, with its connotations of "other," "different," or "ethnic" (e.g., Western vs. non-Western); and the nominal amalgam appears to emphasize the musicology component over the ethnological (or anthropological) rather than the interaction of musicology and ethnology on equal terms. While no single term is entirely satisfactory, "music ethnology" (like "dance ethnology") at least has the virtue of clarity as well as suggesting a more equable balance between the disciplines.

What's in a name? Terminology aside, a good general bibliography for ethnomusicology has not existed since the 1960s. As the present work reminds us, the last comprehensive bibliography, Jaap Kunst's *Ethnomusicology*, and its supplement, were published in 1959 and 1960 respectively. Bruno Nettl compiled a selective list of reference works in 1961 (revised in 1967), but it was relatively modest and included only leading reference works. There is a need for a bibliography aimed at both the lay reader and the professional teacher: the former needs a useful introduction to the discipline, the latter a practical tool for the classroom. The first publication in this series, then, aims to fill a gap, in particular for North American and English-language work.

Because of her long experience as Head (1961-74) and then Director (1974-84) of the Ethnomusicology Archive at U.C.L.A., Ann Briegleb Schuursma brings a close knowledge of the material to the present publication. Dr. Schuursma completed her B.A. in Music at U.C.L.A. (1956), then gained an M.L.S. in Library Science from the University of Southern California (1958). After a short period as Assistant Head in the College Library, U.C.L.A. (1958-61), she became Head of the newly formed Ethnomusicology Archive.

In 1969 Dr. Schuursma began her studies of Romanian folk music with the aid of a Fulbright-Hays Research Grant and continued her fieldwork there with a grant from the International Research and Exchanges Board (1971-72). She completed her field research in Cluj-Napoca in 1978-79, again with the help of a Fulbright-Hays Grant. Her dissertation on the winter solstice *colindat* ritual and its music as practiced in five villages of Valea Muresului (Hunedoara Province, Southwestern Romania), was finished at U.C.L.A. in 1987.

The usefulness of Dr. Schuursma's new research and information guide will be readily apparent. She has arranged the contents in an easily accessible format, including chapters on (1) the history of ethnomusicology, (2) theory and method, (3) fieldwork methods, (4) musical analysis, and (perhaps of special value), (5) sources from related disciplines. A name and a subject index are indispensable parts of the guide, as is her short introduction on the development of ethnomusicology. The annotations are carefully devised to convey the gist of each work, and Dr. Schuursma's preface specifies clearly the limitations she has imposed on the material. While bibliographies of any kind are bound to be outdated as soon as they appear, the present one boldly supports Richard Crawford's assertion that without bibliography (discography, filmography) there can be no real scholarship.

James Porter, *Editor*
The Garland Library of Music Ethnology

PREFACE

Without bibliography there can be no real scholarship.
—Richard Crawford (1985:4)[1]

Scope and Objectives

The purpose of this bibliography is to supply a guide to the most significant and representative recent literature in the field of ethnomusicology. Certain limitary factors regarding time and subject have dictated its scope. Coverage is general rather than culture/area specific, and it is selective. It spans a restricted time period beginning in 1960 and continuing to the present. The field of ethnomusicology is taken generally in its broad meaning of "the study of music in culture" (Merriam) or "as culture" (Herndon) and is specifically applied to the American scene.

Several reasons compelled me to view the work as a general bibliography rather than a culture specific one. First of all, there is no general bibliography for ethnomusicological research for the period after 1960. The last general bibliography, Jaap Kunst's *Ethnomusicology*, and its supplement, were published in 1959 and 1960 respectively.[2] A selective list of reference works was compiled by Bruno Nettl in 1961 and later revised in 1967 (see item 119 below). It was, however, a very modest work and as its title indicates, contained only the leading reference works in the field.

Second, an increasing number of bibliographies specializing in a particular music culture are being published or are at least in the

---

[1]Crawford, Richard. *Studying American Music*. Institute for Studies in American Music Special Publications No. 3. Brooklyn, New York: Institute for Studies in American Music, 1985.

[2]Kunst, Jaap. *Ethnomusicology; a Study . . . to Which is Added a Bibliography*. The Hague: Nijhoff, 1959; *Supplement*, 1960.

planning phase. In most cases they have been prepared by area specialists who are better qualified to do this work than generalists.

Third, a good general bibliography aimed at both lay persons and scholars is perhaps the most important need of the field at present. An enormous amount of literature has sprung up over the past thirty years but tools for bibliographic control are still limited.[1]

Part of the growing amount of literature comes from scholarly institutions and organizations that have begun issuing their own ethnomusicological publications (e.g., the *Selected Reports in Ethnomusicology* series from U.C.L.A. and the *Special Series* of the Society for Ethnomusicology). Furthermore, certain publishers have put into place their own ethnomusicological series (e.g., the *Cambridge Studies in Ethnomusicology* by Cambridge University Press). Several new series are, at the time of this writing, in preparation (e.g., *Chicago Studies in Ethnomusicology* by the University of Chicago Press and *Recent Researches in the Oral Traditions of Music* from A-R Editions, Inc., Madison, Wisconsin).

Additionally, large encyclopedic works have recently added to both the quantity and quality of the literature, e.g., the twenty-volume *The New Grove Dictionary of Music and Musicians* (London: Macmillan, 1980) and its various offshoots. Plans are afoot for several more encyclopedic and multi-volume works that will increase the amount of printed words a hundredfold. One of these is historically oriented—the UNESCO/IMC project *The Universe of Music: A History* (formerly *Music in the Life of Man*); the other—the Garland *Encyclopedia of World Music*—takes an ethnomusicological perspective.

A highly selective bibliography is needed, then, to guide an initiate through the published quantity of material in English. Two strategies assisted me in the selection process. One was the use of reading lists

---

[1] For example, the Current Bibliography section of *Ethnomusicology* journal (referred to as "CB and D" when it added discography) has been up to now the singular, relatively easy, major source for maintaining bibliographic control. The escalating quantity of material can be measured by comparing various years of "CB." For example, in the May 1963 issue (compiled by Bruno Nettl, overall editor in its early days) there are a modest six pages. In the Spring/Summer 1989 issue (compiled for many years by CB and D special editor Joe Hickerson and now by Jennifer Post) there are approximately seventeen. The necessity to become even more selective has developed hand-in-hand with the increase of the literature.

obtained from leading United States institutions where ethno-musicology is taught. In response to written requests to over twenty-five teachers of ethnomusicology, I received course lists of recommended and/or required readings. Particularly useful were those lists prepared for introductory courses in theory and methodology, fieldwork theory and method, and transcription and analysis.

The second strategy was to draw from my long experience as an ethnomusicology librarian and archivist at U.C.L.A. All items in the present work have been personally examined, initially in order to make the selection (many were discarded) and ultimately to compose the annotations.

The choice of a restricted time frame stems from a variety of reasons. The first is a personal one. During the past three decades I was immersed in ethnomusicological literature, both as a librarian and as a graduate student. Selecting books for the U.C.L.A. Music Library for almost twenty-five years gave me the experience which has been put to a new productive use.

Another restrictive time factor is that the last three decades have seen remarkable growth and development in the discipline. This has come about within a relatively short span of time. Comparison of literature from the 1960s with that from the 1980s reveals a dramatic difference in ways of thinking and treatment of subject matter. This bibliography provides the reader, I hope, with an opportunity to observe this remarkable period of growth in ethnomusicology.

Specific Limitations

Within the parameters of selection it may be helpful to mention what has not been included in this work regarding both subjects and types of materials. Furthermore, it is not intended as a bibliography of area studies although such items are scattered throughout. Because the work has more to do with overall issues, a separate section for area studies was deemed inappropriate. Readers may wish to consult the subject index for references to specific area studies.

The following subjects were excluded from the bibliography: popular music (except the study of Peter Manuel) and dance (except the methodological studies of Hanna, Kaeppler and Royce). These subjects are covered, on the whole, by their own specialized bibliographies.[1] Moreover, they are such enormous subjects by themselves that it would have been impossible to incorporate them in this modest work. Although organology was originally planned as a main section it quickly became apparent that this was impractical because it is too intertwined with historical musicology. It deserves a bibliography of its own.

Types of printed materials also excluded are: reviews (except for an occasional mention in an annotation of a book), newspaper articles, recording notes (except for Lomax), and doctoral dissertations and master's theses (exceptions include several dissertations which were never published as books). Reprints or republications of materials written before 1960 have likewise been excluded.[2]

Finally, this is basically a bibliography of English-language items because it is directed toward an American readership that does not easily read foreign languages. I do not in any way mean to imply that scholarship in English is better than in any other language. The decision was simply a pragmatic one. In several cases where English translations of French or German works are in print, these are included.

Organization

The bibliography has been divided into five main categories representing important aspects of ethnomusicology: (1) history of the field, (2) theory and methodology, (3) fieldwork theory and method, (4) musical analysis, and (5) sources from related fields. Preceding the bibliography is an introduction that serves as a brief overview of developments in ethnomusicology over the past thirty years.

The first section of the bibliography deals with history of the field. As Alan Merriam once remarked, there has been a dearth of research

---

[1] For example, Roman Iwaschkin. *Popular Music: A Reference Guide*. New York: Garland, 1986.

[2] The reader's attention is directed to the *Garland Library of Readings in Ethnomusicology* [7 volumes] (New York: Garland, 1990). It provides a variety of selected essays dating from the nineteenth century to the mid-1980s. Many of the articles in this bibliography are reprinted there. The reader is advised to consult the contents, particularly for earlier items, before conducting a time-consuming library search.

and writing on the history of ethnomusicology and I have therefore devoted a whole category to it.[1] For pre-1960 history, see the Introduction to Jaap Kunst's *Ethnomusicology*, pp. 1-66.

The second grouping concerns theory and method and is the central focus of the work. In it are included the major works that reflect the overall research activity during this period. Much of this literature concerns specific area studies, but the criterion for including a particular item has depended more on the theoretical or methodological background of the work.

Fieldwork Method and Technique, the third category, covers theoretical as well as practical aspects. It cites works that plan a research project, carry it out and analyze it afterward. Recent writing tends to be remarkably candid in describing field experiences. For the most part, sources about the purely technical aspects of fieldwork, such as types of equipment and field techniques for handling camera or audio, have not been included. Musical Analysis, the topic of Part IV, includes a variety of methodological approaches.

The idea for Part V, Sources from Related Fields, came from one particularly expansive reading list that I received from a colleague. Originally meant to reflect influences from diverse areas of anthropology, the section broadened out to include sociology, folklore, linguistics and psychology. Because ethnomusicologists have begun to explore issues of gender and ideology, as well as of self and emotion in relation to culture and music, I found it particularly useful to include some sources from related social science fields in this section. I remind the reader that Part V represents only a sampling of the literature and should by no means be considered definitive.

Format and Annotations

Bibliographic format follows "Style A" from the *Chicago Manual of Style* and has striven to be as accurate and consistent as possible.

---

[1] An important collection of essays on the history of ethnomusicology resulting from the conference, "Ideas, Concepts, and Personalities in the History of Ethnomusicology," was published too late to be included in this bibliography: Bruno Nettl and Philip V. Bohlman, editors. *Comparative Musicology and Anthropology of Music: Essays on the History of Ethnomusicology.* Chicago: University of Chicago Press, 1991.

Titles can give inadequate, even misleading, information from which to determine a work's content. Annotations, therefore, often supplement information not evident in titles. They are factual rather than evaluative and appear in summary form. Additional information places each source in a more holistic perspective with regard to developments in the field. In the end, however, readers will want to make their own selection, and annotations are meant to assist this process.

As much as possible I have sought to include items that are still in print (as of the date of this writing). In the few cases where this is not true, "o.p." for "out-of-print" is mentioned in brackets at the end of the bibliographic information.[1]

Cross-references are indicated whenever a source could potentially appear in more than one category. The full citation and annotation are given only once, when the item is cited the first time. Subsequent inclusions are indicated by a See Also reference.

Indexes

Because the bibliographic items are dispersed throughout the five different sections of this work, two indexes have been provided to assist in ready reference: a name index, and a subject index that includes geographical places and ethnographic cultural groups. In developing the subject index, I have applied my knowledge of indexing techniques.[2] Cross-references have been provided where necessary.

---

[1] See p. ix, footnote 2 concerning the *Garland Library of Readings*.
[2] See Schuursma, Ann. "Subject Access to Sound Recordings in Ethnomusicology: a Timely Need." *Discourse in Ethnomusicology III: Essays in Honor of Frank J. Gillis*, ed. by Nancy Cassell McEntire, 151-65. Bloomington: Ethnomusicology Publications Group, 1991.

ACKNOWLEDGMENTS

Compiling a bibliography means developing a close relationship with one or more libraries. In Rotterdam, where I now live, there is no library collection concentrating on ethnomusicology such as I was accustomed to at U.C.L.A. Sources are scattered throughout the Netherlands. For this reason I came to know my new colleagues and their library collections very well. I would like to express my thanks and appreciation to them all, especially the Erasmus University library in Rotterdam. I am particularly grateful to Marie-José Vlaanderen, philosophy bibliographer, and Maryann Meijer, for their assistance in on-line catalog searching, and Gerard Mazee, of the interlibrary loan section of the Circulation Department, who worked miracles to locate difficult materials.

In the United States I worked extensively at both the U.C.L.A. Music Library and the Ethnomusicology Archive. I especially appreciate the friendship and professional support given by my colleague and friend, Marsha Berman. At the Harvard Loeb Music Library, Millard Irion, Public Services Librarian, and Michael Ochs, head of the Music Library, deserve my thanks for their help.

For review copies of certain items requested directly from their publishers, I wish to acknowledge the following: the ICTM Secretariat, Indiana University Press, Kent State University Press, San Diego State University Press, Schirmer Books and Temple University Press.

It took much more than libraries and publishers to complete this bibliography, however. Soliciting reading lists from colleagues in teaching institutions resulted in responses essential to the selection process. In addition, several colleagues spent valuable time discussing their assessment of literature representative of the period covered. Some helped by reading early proofs or by sending hard-to-get photocopies of articles or books. In this regard I wish to thank Marsha Berman, Dieter Christensen, Charlotte Frisbie, Barbara Hampton, Charlotte Heth, Roderic Knight, Nancy McEntire, James Porter, Jihad

Racy, Tim Rice, Don Roberts, Anthony Seeger, Kay Kaufman Shelemay, Ruth Stone, Elizabeth Tatar, Jeff Titon, and Bonnie Wade.

A word of thanks to Kathy Barrett who put the final touches on the computer-generated text, and to series editor, James Porter, who kept me in line with encouraging words and helpful suggestions.

Last, but by far not the least, I gratefully and lovingly express my appreciation to Rolf Schuursma for giving me his very special personal encouragement and professional support.

As author and compiler I take full responsibility for the contents of this bibliography and the opinions expressed. I welcome information about omissions and corrections from readers. If a revised edition is forthcoming (dependent on the energies and resources of both publisher and author), such information will of course be invaluable.

INTRODUCTION

A Brief Overview of Recent Ethnomusicological Research

A century or more ago, when ethnomusicology (then called comparative musicology) was beginning to emerge as a subject in its own right, it was regarded as a product of one or the other of its parent disciplines, musicology and ethnology. Scholars working in these disciplines were occupied with their particular subject within the parameters of the respective discipline: musicologists were concerned with the music product itself, whereas ethnologists were more interested in the social context of music. Only in the past three decades have the two disciplines developed in the direction of a more comprehensive and integrated approach through the growth of ethnomusicology.

The purpose of this brief overview is to note major developments in American ethnomusicology as they are reflected in the bibliography. Recent directions are described chronologically, and this is followed by a discussion of influences on ethnomusicology from other disciplines. I include both influences from social science fields, mainly those of anthropology, ethnology, folklore, linguistics and psychology, and the relationship and mutual exchange of ideas between musicology and ethnomusicology.

For a more thorough discussion of the main "issues and concepts" that have engaged the field, I refer the reader to the comprehensive study by Bruno Nettl, *The Study of Ethnomusicology: Twenty-Nine Issues and Concepts* (item 16). This work is recommended for anyone wishing to become familiar with the field of ethnomusicology as a whole; for another more recent book on the history of ethnomusicology edited by Nettl and Bohlman, see footnote, p. xiii of the Preface. Selected articles in *The New Grove Dictionary of Music and Musicians* can also be used as introductory sources.

Issues and concepts in ethnomusicology can be difficult for the beginner to grasp, not least because of the ambiguities in the word itself (the "ethno-" prefix, particularly). In the Preface it was noted that the past three decades have seen a remarkable period of growth and development in the discipline, and many factors have contributed to this. As noted above, the discipline had already been evolving in two different directions simultaneously because of its origins in ethnology and musicology; theory and method, therefore, were often pursued along rather different lines. A feeling of inadequacy and insecurity in developing research methods sometimes caused ethnomusicologists to look outside their own discipline for inspiration. Yet the move from ethnomusicology's status as an interdisciplinary "field" to a full-fledged "discipline" can be traced directly to the evolution of a distinctive "ethnomusicological" literature during the post-World War II period.

Recent Developments in Ethnomusicology

At the end of the Second World War the curtain rose on a new era in ethnomusicological "education" and research. Musicologists and anthropologists increased their study of non-Western and folk music, and Western musicologists recognized that analysis of musical cultures other than their own (Western concert music) was necessary to open up cross-cultural understanding and avoid colonialist stereotyping. The result was the inclusion of non-Western and folk music in their curricula, an especially problematic development because of the dearth of qualified teachers. The situation was ripe for establishing university programs in which ethnomusicology would be a specialization and where future teachers could receive adequate training. To fill this need, programs in both musicology and anthropology began to grow at universities such as Columbia, Wesleyan, Indiana, Illinois, Northwestern and the University of California, Los Angeles.

The sixties

By the beginning of the 1960s ethnomusicology was poised to grow out of its childhood and into its adolescence. Almost a hundred years after the pioneers Alexander Ellis, Carl Stumpf, and Erich von Hornbostel had begun to develop comparative musicology, a principal concern remained: how to create a discipline in its own right. In Europe it had emerged as a field of musicology (after Guido Adler), while in America it had its origins as a field of anthropology (following Franz Boas). George Herzog, a pupil of Erich von Hornbostel, and Melville Herskovits had already been teaching before the war at American universities. Later, in the sixties, their students branched out and started or enlarged programs at other universities (e.g., Alan Merriam, who had studied at Northwestern University with Herskovits, began the program at Indiana University, and Bruno Nettl, who studied at Indiana University under Herzog, was primarily responsible for the program at the University of Illinois).

A rather different kind of ethnomusicology program began at the University of California at Los Angeles. There Mantle Hood, who in the mid-fifties had studied under Jaap Kunst at the University of Amsterdam, put into practice his ideas about bi-musicality by setting up study/performing groups in non-Western and folk music. Later in the decade his students spread this practice to other U.S. universities: William Malm at the University of Michigan, Robert Garfias at the University of Washington, and Robert Brown at Wesleyan University.

In the prevailing atmosphere of positivism, the 1960s was a time to be as "scientific" and "objective" as possible. Theoretical research models began to develop, the first significant statement being that of Merriam (item 11). Other models—of method, of context, of performance, of the field—would follow later, for example, by Herndon, Gourlay, Rice, Feld and Nketia (see subject index under *models*).

Particularly important to making musical study as "scientific" as possible was the process of musical analysis. Machines were developed to assist in analysis and transcription, among them the Melograph at U.C.L.A. (the brainchild of Charles Seeger, see item 313, especially the article by Moore), in Jerusalem (Cohen and Katz, item 284), and the Mona and Polly machines developed at Uppsala University in Sweden (items 276 and 314).

This was also a time to define ethnomusicology and to forecast the direction of the field. In this endeavor anthropologists like Merriam and musicologists like Hood often disagreed. Immigrant scholars like Mieczyslaw Kolinski, the last of the "armchair ethnomusicologists," preferred to stay rooted in the earlier concept of comparative musicology as developed by Hornbostel and to describe and analyze the music itself.

A new concept and method, termed Cantometrics, was developed by Alan Lomax during this period (see items 93 and 94). Fieldwork put an end to "armchair ethnomusicology" and began prescribing structured methods. Film began to be used as a valuable supplement in fieldwork and documentation in the analysis of complex musical activity, but did not necessarily replace tape recording.

During the sixties, other areas of research and writing included concern about the relationship between speech and song (George List, item 90), acculturation (Klaus Wachsmann, item 192), and biography as a method for studying a subject (begun by folklorists such as Henry Glassie et al. [item 372] and Roger Abrahams, and followed in the seventies by, for example, the ethnomusicologists Charlotte Frisbie and David McAllester, item 114).

The second decade

In the seventies the influence of linguistics on the analysis of music was significant, a prominent example being the semiotic approach developed by Jean-Jacques Nattiez. Researchers at the Groupe de Recherches en Sémiologie Musicale at the University of Montreal, established by Nattiez, aimed at greater objectivity in musical analysis.

Some preferred to apply linguistic methods in other ways and looked to transformational and generative grammar as developed by Chomsky and others. This was reflected in the writings of John Blacking (deep structures, item 33), Steven Feld (item 56), and Charles Boilès (relationship between language and music, item 45), and Judith and Alton Becker (mainly in reference to Indonesian music, item 28). Harold Powers, summing up, felt that language models could contribute fundamentally to musical disciplines (item 308). Still others such as Marcia Herndon applied cognitive theory to musical analysis (item 289).

Research design and fieldwork method became increasingly important. The behavioral fields of cultural anthropology, ethnology, sociology, folklore, and psychology often provided model examples. The insider/outsider approach as articulated by Paul Berliner (item 30),

Kenneth Gourlay (item 62), and Charles Keil (item 85) derived in great part from the etic/emic standpoint for the description of language behavior developed by the linguist Kenneth Pike (item 430).

Fieldwork was especially influenced by methods from folklore and anthropology. Participant observer methods were used by Frisbie (item 60), among others, and the topic of the ethics of fieldwork merited special sessions at Society for Ethnomusicology meetings. Video began to replace film as a fieldwork medium.

The study of urban ethnomusicology emerged and became part of the ethnomusicology curriculum at Columbia University. Adelaida Reyes Schramm was one of the first to work extensively in this area (items 142–45).

At least two notation systems designed to assist the transcription of rhythmic units were 1) James Koetting's for complex African drum patterns, T.U.B.S. (Time Unit Box System) (item 297), and N.U.T.S. (Nominal Units of Time System), introduced by Nazir Jairazbhoy (item 292). Others continued working with the various transcription machine aids such as the several Melographs designed in Israel (item 284), in the United States (item 313) and the monophonic and polyphonic "melody-writers" in Sweden (items 276 and 314).

Interest in conceptual models, and in performance, began to grow as, for example, the model based on multiple performances of the same song by one singer offered by James Porter (items 133 and 134). Other issues included the study of musical style especially identifying processes of change, the meaning in music, musical values, and aesthetics. The subject of universals in music warranted a special session at an S.E.M. conference which resulted in the publication of several articles.

The third decade

In 1980 *The New Grove Dictionary of Music and Musicians* drew considerable attention to its inclusion of ethnomusicological subjects. This was the first time world music topics were approached, in an encyclopedic work, from an analytical perspective other than that of the Western classical tradition. Although the "art/folk music" division in describing some musical cultures is unsatisfactory, the entries often reflect a newly strengthened, mutually rewarding relationship between musicology and ethnomusicology as well as influences from other intellectual fields. This has continued in the later literature of the decade.

The decade's redefinition of goals and methods called for new models of research, and at this point the significance of cognitive anthropology became apparent. Some ethnomusicologists turned for inspiration to writers in other disciplines, e.g., Timothy Rice to Clifford Geertz (item 148). A general move away from "objectivity" began to emerge. Deeper analysis of field experiences appeared (e.g., Steven Feld, item 57, and Anthony Seeger, item 257). The study of symbolic systems often involved deciphering the metaphoric process (Feld, items 55, 57, and 58).

Gender studies, much of it coming from the women's movement, became an issue that included the relationship of gender to music, and to power (Keeling, item 83; Koskoff, item 400; Robertson, item 151; Sugarman, item 183). Social organization and the musician was a concern for several researchers such as D. Neuman (items 124 and 125) and E. Henry (items 68 and 69). The ecological perspective concerned at least one writer (item 84).

The ethnography of musical performance, strongly influenced by folklore studies in performance, was reflected in writings of Béhague (item 29), McLeod and Herndon (item 100), Qureshi (items 139 and 140), and Sugarman (item 183). Folklore was also the inspiration for studies of the fieldworker as performer (Koning, items 231 and 232). Analyzing the music event as an approach came into its own through the work of Ruth Stone and her husband, Verlon (item 265), and borrowed heavily from sociology, anthropology, linguistics as well as folklore.

The informant's musical cognition (Sakata, item 157), music cognition in general (Dowling and Harwood, item 50), and the cognitive nature of musical communication (Hopkins, item 77) also represented influences from psychology and anthropology.

Historical approaches, either as renewal movements in historical studies or as interpretive histories, persisted throughout the decade (Shelemay, item 173). During this time two events took place which focused on history and ethnomusicology, a pre-conference before the S.E.M. Annual Meeting at Ann Arbor, Michigan, and a special conference organized by Bruno Nettl at the University of Illinois (see footnote on p. xiii in Preface).

Influences from Related Fields

It has already been noted that, in order to develop its own theories and methods, ethnomusicology drew upon practices in other disciplines. The extent and nature of the influences of related disciplines upon ethnomusicology have a historical precedent that is worthy of some attention.

In Austria, Guido Adler viewed comparative musicology as a branch of musicology, and this was coupled with an equally strong evolutionary perspective. In America, on the other hand, ethnomusicology grew out of anthropology and reflected the functionalist orientations of Franz Boas.

Contrasting the two "schools" of thought—those of Adler and Boas—the early paradigms were as follows:

(1) In musicology the emphasis was upon nomothetic inquiry (to arrive at acceptable *general* propositions on a subject), and in anthropology on *both* nomothetic and idiographic inquiries (to establish the acceptability of *particular* propositions or statements).

(2) The diachronic approach was used primarily in musicology while both diachronic and synchronic approaches were employed by anthropologists.

(3) Musicologists pursued armchair ethnomusicology while anthropologists placed a strong emphasis on fieldwork.

(4) German ethnomusicology drew scholars from a wide variety of disciplines (Otto Abraham was a physician, for example), while American ethnomusicologists were usually anthropologists.

(5) Both German and American scholars were concerned with oral traditions, although the former focused on non-Western music and studied Western folk musics as survivals while the latter were concerned primarily with American Indian music.

(6) Both schools shared the application of comparative method although the musicologists were interested in large complexes of cultural traits once geographically unified but later dispersed over the world; the anthropologists concentrated on discrete

geographical units showing contiguous distribution of cultural elements.

(7) Although both were involved to some extent in the analysis of music sound, the musicologists considered it a priority.

(8) Both were concerned about the preservation of music.

(9) Only the anthropologists were concerned with the relationship of music to its cultural context.

Later, ethnomusicologists looked to linguistics and folklore for suitable theory and method. A schematic overview of the influences from other disciplines has been detailed (item 7). The main paradigms are shown to be: evolutionism (from anthropology and folklore), diffusionism (from anthropology and folklore), functionalism and structuralism (from anthropology), structural and transformational-generative models (from linguistics), ethnography of communication (from sociolinguistics and information theory), enactment-centered approach (from folklore), the etic/emic dichotomy (from linguistics) and nomothetic revival (from anthropology).

Further clarification of recent developments in the field of anthropology can be gained from Ortner's summary (item 427).

Musicology

A century before the term "ethnomusicology" was introduced by Jaap Kunst (1950), musicology had often included folk music and non-Western music in its studies. In the beginning these studies were closely bound up with nationalistic and religious ideology. Even into the 1980s, some musicologists made no pretense of the fact that they were not very interested in non-Western music except for what it could bring to the study of Western art music.[1]

After World War II, musicology concentrated on traditional research: mainly historical interpretation, with an emphasis on transcription and analysis, and on aesthetics and criticism. Quite

---

[1]One is Joseph Kerman, who devoted an entire chapter to the relationship between ethnomusicology and "cultural musicology" (item 396).

recently, however, it has acknowledged that a more comprehensive, integrated approach is needed in addition to seeing music as an art leading to performance. The three essays of Frank Harrison, Mantle Hood and Claude Palisca (item 381) did much to initiate a new dialogue between the two disciplines.

Links with ethnomusicology have grown especially in the areas of oral transmission of music and the concept of mode. Panels held at the International Musicological Society conference at Berkeley in 1977, for instance, consisted of both musicological and ethnomusicological participants. Discussions after the paper presentations were particularly influential in laying the groundwork for further research and publication. *The New Grove*, which followed shortly, continued this new development.

One musicologist has commented that Harold Powers has shed more light on the meaning of mode in 16th century music than any of the other musicologists who have worked on this problem (item 396). Conversely, the writings of musicologists such as Charles Rosen have been read and absorbed by many ethnomusicologists (item 438).

Most recently there has been a renewed interest in historical subjects in ethnomusicology as well as in areas previously regarded as outside the field, such as Western classical music. Kingsbury and Nettl, for instance, have produced studies using an ethnomusicological approach to a musicological subject.

Certainly, ethnomusicological methods have influenced musicological and other journals appearing during this period. The model set by *Ethnomusicology* is reflected in such publications as *Asian Music* (1968–), *Popular Music and Society* (1972–), *Latin American Music Review* (1980–), and *American Music* (1983–).

Conclusion

The diminishing of description-centered scholarship in favor of analysis, evaluation and interpretation of all sensory data surounding music and its production (including self-analysis by the researcher) characterizes recent ethnomusicological research in America. The search for and use of paradigms from related disciplines greatly accelerated this development. The move away from "objectivity" and "sciencing about music" (Merriam) and the emergence of research models based on phenomenology and its outgrowths in cognate fields (e.g., "cognitive," "interpretive," or "practice" anthropology) are keys to current research.

Ann Schuursma
April 1991

ABBREVIATIONS

ASA	Association of Social Anthropologists
CA	*Current Anthropology*
EM	*Ethnomusicology*; Journal of the Society for Ethnomusicology
ICTM	International Council of Traditional Music (formerly IFMC)
IFMC	International Folk Music Council
LAMR	*Latin American Music Review*
SEM	Society for Ethnomusicology
YTM	*Yearbook for Traditional Music*

Ethnomusicology Research

I. HISTORY OF ETHNOMUSICOLOGY AS A FIELD

1. Baily, John. "John Blacking and His Place in Ethnomusicology." *Yearbook for Traditional Music* 22 (1990):xii-xxi.

   Written by a former graduate student and colleague, this short biographical tribute helps to place Blacking's research and writings in a broader perspective. A chronological list of writings concludes the contribution (it includes many of the items of the bibliography prepared by Alan Marsden in *Ethnomusicology* 34/2:226–70).

2. Bohlman, Philip V. "Traditional Music and Cultural Identity: Persistent Paradigm in the History of Ethnomusicology." *Yearbook for Traditional Music* 20/1 (1988):26–42.

   Re-examination of the intellectual history of ethnomusicology on the occasion of forty years of I.F.M.C./I.C.T.M. Perceives a unity that began in the 18th century and continues today. This unity results from the persistence of paradigms combining two components: traditional music and cultural identity.

3. Christensen, Dieter. "The International Folk Music Council and 'The Americans': On the Effects of Stereotypes on the Institutionalization of Ethnomusicology." *Yearbook for Traditional Music* 20/1 (1988):11–18.

   Considers the preoccupations that arose in the Council's governing body from the juxtaposition of Europeans and Americans; covers the time period 1954–1967.

4. Elbourne, R. P. "The Question of Definition." *Yearbook of the International Folk Music Council* 7, 1975 (1976):9–29.

Concerns the definition of "folk music," particularly the elements in the I.F.M.C. 1955 definition. Complains that existing definitions founder in being too narrowly based on content and form. Discusses two main approaches: one concerned with internal properties, the other with cultural background. Prefers the term "traditional music"—the popular musical expression of a traditional social structure . . . any kind of music, no matter what its origin or content, can become part of a tradition.

5. Etzkorn, K. Peter. "Publications and Their Influence on the Development of Ethnomusicology." *Yearbook for Traditional Music* 20/1 (1988):43–50.

Drawing on his experience as Editor of *Ethnomusicology*, 1985–87, the author reflects on making or performing music and how the scholarly processes of writing or speaking about music may offer insights into the future development of ethnomusicology.

6. Hood, Mantle. *The Ethnomusicologist.* 2nd ed. Kent, Ohio: Kent State University Press, 1982. [Originally published New York: McGraw-Hill, 1971]. Three accompanying 7" discs.

Personal philosophy of a founding father in the development of ethnomusicology programs within university music departments in the U.S. Relates a "living history" of the U.C.L.A. program for the time period, 1954–1974. Especially valuable for information about the Melograph, as invented by Charles Seeger and developed by Michael Moore, and about Hood's unique "invention" of the organogram, a composite ideogram in which he attempts to distinguish the physical and contextual characteristics of musical instruments.

7. Joseph, Rosemary M. F. "Ethnomusicology: Towards the Holistic Study of Music," Parts 1 and 2. *International Council for Traditional Music, UK Chapter Bulletin* 19 (1988):2–42, and 20 (1988):4–19.

Part 1 summarizes developments in the recent history of ethnomusicology, including the search for definition, theory and method. Provides an overview of the application of theory and method from musicology, anthropology, linguistics and folklore, with recent trends and models. In part 2 the author presents and explains her own diagrammatic model, in the form of concentric circles, for a holistic approach to the study of music.

8. Kolinski, Mieczyslaw. "Recent Trends in Ethnomusicology." *Ethnomusicology* 11/1 (Jan. 1967):1–24.

   Refers to the anthropological "wing" of the discipline, which was then emerging in the writings of Merriam and Blacking. Encourages "the comparative musicologist" to continue working on musicological analysis and so broaden the basis of cooperation between the musicological and ethnological branches of ethnomusicology.

9. Krader, Barbara. "Ethnomusicology." In *New Grove Dictionary of Music and Musicians* 6 (1980):275–82.

   An attempt to cover the main developments in the discipline, with a valuable section on history up to World War II. Section on trends since 1950 includes: 1) collection and documentation, 2) transcription and acoustic analysis, 3) classification, systematization and analysis, 4) social function, 5) the historical dimension, 6) ethics, and 7) conclusion. It has, however, certain gaps and does not reflect the more recent anthropological/sociological work of scholars such as Feld, Roseman, or Keil.

10. Marshall, Christopher. "Two Paradigms of Music: A Short History of Ideas in Ethnomusicology." *Cornell Journal of Social Relations* 7 (1972):75–83.

    A clear outline of the history of theory in ethnomusicology and a discussion of how institutional and social history have done a lot to mold and influence that history. Offers suggestions on the role of anthropologists in ethnomusicology and the possibilities for them inherent in the field. Influenced by Merriam's work in its general approach.

11. Merriam, Alan. *The Anthropology of Music*. Evanston, Ill.: Northwestern University Press, 1964.

A "living history" from the major anthropological figure of this time period. Although history is not his prime concern, much historical information is scattered throughout. Written at about the same time as Hood's "Music the Unknown," the work fills a gap from the perspective of anthropology since it was felt at the time that the ethnological aspect of the discipline had not received enough attention. Treats three main aspects: theory, method and technique; concepts and behavior; and problems and results. Valuable for its theoretical model for the study of music and an exposition of how the model works. See the multiple reviews in *CA* 7:217–30.

12. ———. "Ethnomusicology: Discussion and Definition of the Field." *Ethnomusicology* 4/3 (1960):107–14.

Observes the growth of ethnomusicology and compares it with archaeology, old and new. Offers a broad view of the discipline in terms of its being led more and more by cultural anthropology.

13. Nettl, Bruno. "The IFMC/ICTM and the Development of Ethnomusicology in the United States." *Yearbook for Traditional Music* 20/1 (1988):19–25.

May be read together with Christensen's contribution in the same number of the *Yearbook* (item 3). Nettl traces the same subject but from an American rather than a European viewpoint. Considers the 1950 conference in Bloomington, Indiana, a landmark and notes the creation of a distinctively American approach to ethnomusicology. A brief description of the founding of the S.E.M. is included.

14. ———. "Some Aspects of the History of World Music in the Twentieth Century: Questions, Problems, and Concepts." *Ethnomusicology* 22/1 (Jan. 1978):123–36.

Takes as its point of departure the notion of the 20th century as a period of musical homogenization. Given the fact that there is an increased availability of many musics to most people, the paper centers on the reactions of other cultures to the introduction and importation of Western music and musical thought. Essay's purpose is to seek a framework for the systematic and comparative study of change resulting from the impact of Western music and musical thought on the world's population.

15. ———. "The State of Research in Ethnomusicology, and Recent Developments." *Current Musicology* 20 (1975):67–78.

Originally prepared for the 23rd conference of the I.F.M.C. (now I.C.T.M.), Regensburg, 1975, and titled "The State of Research in Orally Transmitted Music." Notes difficulty is adequately controlling the amount of information and literature in ethnomusicology in order to assess its general state. Identifies and criticizes descriptive and analytical problems of the past 10–15 years, the present (1975) and the future. Discusses definition of the discipline, communication between scholars, regression to comparative studies, decline of interest in transcription, introduction of semiotics into analysis and description, new perspectives on musical repertories, a move back to historical studies, new attitudes to fieldwork and methods (mainly ethics), the influence from other disciplines, redefinition of categories, and a need for more theory. Instructive to compare with Merriam's article on the state of the discipline at the same time (in the same journal issue).

16. ———. *The Study of Ethnomusicology: Twenty-Nine Issues and Concepts.* Urbana, Ill.: University of Illinois Press, 1983.

Valuable for its historical perspective on present and past developments. Discusses a number of central issues and problems in relation to the early 80s. Main sections include the comparative study of music, the study of music in culture, the study of music in the field, and the study of the world's musics. Postlude, "The Grand March" (pp. 355–61), poses some questions about where ethnomusicology has been and its possible future direction. Excels as a summary of the discipline though at times avoids critical evaluation. Feld describes it as a combination of introduction, retrospect, overview, and state-of-the-field of ethnomusicology as well as a fine teaching source (*LAMR* 7/1:375–8). Robertson recommends it for students with minimal training in the field who seek a guideline for understanding the new world of literature available (*EM* 29:377–80). Jairazbhoy (*JAMS* 42:625–39 remarks that the book exposes the reader to the variety of approaches and analytical components in ethnomusicology, many of which still remain to be explored in Western musicology; while it provides conceptual challenges to specialists it may be too diffuse for those working in the related areas of anthropology, folklore and the like.

17. Seeger, Charles. "United States of America, II. Folk Music." *The New Grove Dictionary of Music and Musicians* 9 (1980):436–47.

   Describes, in five sections, the concept and study of folk music in relation to the three predominant culture communities: Amerindian, Euro-American and Afro-American.

18. Wachsmann, Klaus. "Folk Music." *The New Grove Dictionary of Music and Musicians* 6 (1980):693.

   Identifies the term as more meaningful in Europe and America than elsewhere. Definition as made by I.F.M.C. in 1955 is quoted as well as the *New Grove* article on U.S. Folk Music by Seeger (item 17). Notes the influence of social anthropologists in S.E.M. Emphasizes oral transmission but casts doubt on the belief that folk music has a stylistic identity of its own.

19. Wild, Stephen. "In Memoriam—Alan P. Merriam (1923–1980)." *Ethnomusicology* 26/1 (Jan. 1982):91–8.

   An assessment of Merriam's place in the history of ethnomusicology, mainly as a teacher and advisor. Comments particularly on Merriam's lectures given at Sydney University in 1976 where he was preoccupied with "what is ethnomusicology?" Also mentions what Merriam later considered as weaknesses in his own work.

II. THEORY AND METHOD IN
ETHNOMUSICOLOGY

20. Ames, David W. "A Socio-Cultural View of Hausa Musical Activity." In *The Traditional Artist in African Societies,* edited by Warren d'Azevedo, 128–61. Bloomington: Indiana University Press, 1973; reprinted 1989.

   With the discovery that Hausa do not conceive of musical activity as we do in the West, author classifies the music makers, non-professional and professional, according to the activity for which they perform. Emphasis is on the performer and his perception of the music he performs as well as the context.

21. ———— and Anthony V. King. *Glossary of Hausa Music and its Social Contexts.* Evanston: Northwestern University Press, 1971.

   Terms are listed alphabetically under their Hausa form; focus is on Zaria and Katsina. Grouped according to instruments and their parts, professional performers, patrons, occasions and music performance. The work is, however, more a shorthand ethnography of musical life than an esoteric list of specialized terms. Reviewed and recommended by Fremont E. Besmer in *EM* 16/3:543–4.

22. Apel, Willi, ed. *Harvard Dictionary of Music.* 2nd ed. Cambridge, Mass.: Harvard University Press, 1969. o.p.

   For its time (it may have paved the way for the *New Grove*) this revised and expanded edition reflects the growth of musicology as a field. Ethnomusicology gained considerable ground as seen in the contributions of Nettl, Morton, McAllester, Zonis, Maceda, Hood, Brandel, Pian, Tran Van Khe and W. Kaufmann.

23. Baily, John. "Anthropological and Psychological Approaches to the Study of Music Theory and Musical Cognition." *Yearbook for Traditional Music* 20/1 (1988):114–24.

Proposes a way into the problem of the cognitive role of verbalized music theory by examining the part played by oral notation in learning and performance. Shows how two musical cultures, North India and Afghanistan, use the same music theory but with different cognition. In Afghanistan it is mainly a representational model, while in India it serves an operational role.

24. ———. *Music of Afghanistan; Professional Musicians of the City of Herat.* Cambridge: Cambridge University Press, 1988.

Focuses on male hereditary professional musicians and makes comparisons with amateurs, women, and rural performers. A unique study because soon after the author's research in the 1970s, the area became devastated by warfare. Reviewed by Slobin (*EM* 34:308–9) as a comprehensive account of a professional musicians' group within a single urban area. Review points to the clear, detailed, and concise writing and its well-informed quality as an important factor in the book's internal lucidity. Recommended as a companion volume to Veronica Doubleday's *Three Women of Herat* (London: Jonathan Cape, 1988). Zeranska-Kominek's review (*YTM* 22:143–4) comments that Baily's committed, occasionally emotional attitude towards his subject, together with his data and disciplined presentation of scholarly arguments, make it a valuable contribution.

25. Becker, Howard S. "Ethnomusicology and Sociology: A Letter to Charles Seeger." *Ethnomusicology* 33/2 (Spring/Summer 1989): 275–85.

In this 1988 Seeger Memorial lecture a sociologist offers insights into how sociology might contribute to ethnomusicology: to help narrow down the broad scope of studying music in context and to observe the effects of social organization on the content and performance of music.

26. Becker, Judith. "Is Western Art Music Superior?" *Musical Quarterly* 72/3 (1986):341–59.

Argues that, among musicologists, music educators, and even some ethnomusicologists there is a strong belief that Western European art music is superior to all other musics. A few exceptions are allowed: the classical and art music of Iran and India, and even gamelan music of Indonesia. Conceptual foundations consist of three axioms involving naturalness, complexity, and meaningfulness. Remarks are based upon what the author considers faulty thinking underlying this widespread belief. Concludes that each should be studied and understood on its own terms. Illustrates with examples of South African musical bow, Flathead song creation, initiation chant from Benin, 'Are'are panpipe ensembles, and Kaluli *gisalo* songs.

27. ———. "Western Influence in Gamelan Music." *Asian Music* 3/1 (1972):3–9.

Despite the absence of the more obvious Western influences— e.g., pop tunes, diatonic scales—the impact of technology and Western concepts are shown to have become increasingly widespread. Music notation based on European models, which began in the second half of the 19th century, is common practice and has affected certain aspects of gamelan playing, notably regional styles. Radio and gramophone recordings work to imitate the court styles of Surakarta and Jogjakarta, to the detriment of regional styles. Single microphone placement, usually in front of the female singer, has altered the system of relationships among the musical lines. The composition of new gamelan music has also become important.

28. ——— and Alton Becker. "A Musical Icon: Power and Meaning in Javanese Gamelan Music." In *The Sign in Music and Literature,* edited by Wendy Steiner, 203–15. Austin: University of Texas Press, 1981.

Following Kenneth Burke, the authors define iconicity as finding the image of something in another realm of a given culture (e.g., kinship in nature). In answering the question of what makes a particular kind of music "powerful," they use Javanese gamelan music to show striking similarities between musical structure and the Javanese cosmic/calendric realm, as well as in the realm of dramatic plot in the shadow play. They conclude that musical systems are always more than organized sounds and often the way a specific people understand and relate to the phenomenal world.

29. Béhague, Gerard, ed. *Performance Practice: Ethnomusicological Perspectives.* Contributions· in Intercultural and Comparative Studies, no. 12. Westport: Greenwood, 1984.

    A collection of five essays on Indian classical, African, U.S. (fiddling), and Afro-Brazilian musics. The predominant theme is that the study of music performance as an event and a process, and of the resulting performance practices or products, should concentrate on the actual musical and extra-musical behavior of the participants. The rules or codes of performance are therefore defined by the community for a specific context or occasion. Important for the ethnography of performance as well as event analysis. Reviewed by Herndon in *EM* 30/2:346–7 as a valiant effort in redefining the term "performance practice."

30. Berliner, Paul Franklin. *The Soul of Mbira: Music and Traditions of the Shona People of Zimbabwe.* Perspectives on Southern Africa, 26. Berkeley: University of California Press, 1978, 1981.

    Purpose is to draw attention to the use, particularly among the Shona people of Zimbabwe, of the *mbira*, an instrument which the author considers a uniquely African contribution to the world of music. Analyzes mbira music in its broad cultural context from an interactive viewpoint. With appendices of song texts in Shona and English, absolute tunings, how to build and play a Shona Karimba, and five notated pieces with tablature of author's own design (coordinates with author's commercially available recording). Version of the author's Ph.D. dissertation from Wesleyan University (1974). Gourlay remarks that it is not only the most complete account of its kind and for its time but is also a landmark in ethnomusicological literature (*EM* 14:128–9).

31. Blacking, John. "Can Musical Universals Be Heard?" *World of Music* 19/1–2 (1977)[1979]:14–22.

    Considers musical processes, rather than the musical products, vital to the discussion of universals in music. Feels that the musical and social aspects of musical communication are the only real basis for a useful theory of musical universals. Concludes that much research needs to be done before we can begin to speak of musical universals, or near-universals, or even be assured of the sharing of musical experience within circumscribed regions.

32. ———. "Challenging the Myth of 'Ethnic' Music: First Performances of a New Song in an African Oral Tradition, 1961." *Yearbook for Traditional Music* 21 (1989):17–24.

In reporting on the social context and musical background of the first two performances of a new composition by Ida Sakala of the Ng'oma clan (western Zambia), the author proposes that creation always involves the individual, whether or not a tradition records the composer's identity. The song texts reflecting one woman's personal song of sorrow were accepted as very beautiful and unexpectedly new.

33. ———. "Deep and Surface Structures in Venda Music." *Yearbook of the International Folk Music Council* 3, 1971 (1972):91–108.

One of the first statements to analyze music composition and performance in terms of cognitive processes. The author emphasizes that knowing what music really entails as an expression of human behavior is vital.

34. ———. *How Musical is Man?* The John Danz Lectures. Seattle: University of Washington Press, 1973. Accompanying 7" tape recording.

A much-quoted piece of writing by one of the most influential anthropologists-ethnomusicologists of our time. Bases discussion on his fieldwork with the Venda people of South Africa and his experiences studying Western music, especially the piano literature. Holds out hope for a deeper understanding of all music as a result of the discovery of structural relationships between music and social life. Believes that in order to know how musical man is we must be able to describe exactly what happens in any piece of music as well as what happens to the human beings who make the music. Music is a synthesis of cognitive processes present in culture and in the human body: the forms it takes, and the effects it has on people, are generated by the social experiences of human bodies in different cultural environments. Extramusical processes should be included in the analysis of music, such as historical, political, philosophical or rational (in terms of acoustical laws). Shows concern with both surface and deep structures of musical analysis. Presents a model for music making analysis in terms of a "unified theory of cognition, society, culture, and creativity" (pp. 99–100). Reviewed critically by Herndon (*EM* 19:143–5) as more ontological, metaphysical, and psychological than formally logical: "an intensely personal statement."

35.   ———. "Identifying Processes of Musical Change." *World of Music* 28/1 (1986):3–15.

Believes that musical and cultural changes are the result of decisions made by individuals about music-making and music, or about social and cultural practice, on the basis of their experiences and their attitudes towards them. Musical changes may signal far-reaching changes in society and may precede and forecast other changes in a society.

36.   ———. "The Problem of 'Ethnic' Perceptions in the Semiotics of Music." In *The Sign in Music and Literature*, edited by Wendy Steiner, 184–94. Austin: University of Texas Press, 1981.

Calls for the study of processes of musical conceptualization by ethnomusicologists and stresses two issues: 1) multiple perceptions of musical structure should be taken into account in arriving at an explanation of the musical product, and 2) analysis of the creative process, particularly performance. Suggests that music is a special mode of communication, the analysis of which should discover what is peculiar to musical behavior and distinct from other behaviors in the society under study.

37.   ———. "Some Problems of Theory and Method in the Study of Musical Change." *Yearbook of the International Folk Music Council* 9, 1977 (1978):1–26.

Draws attention to the need for a comprehensive theory of music and music-making, and for studies that seek to distinguish *musical* change analytically from other kinds of change, and radical change from variation and innovation within a flexible system. Author emphasizes that we need much more data on cognitive processes at all levels in both the social and musical aspects of music-making before we can locate the critical moments of cognitive change that constitute musical change.

38. ———. "The Value of Music in Human Experience." *Yearbook of the International Folk Music Council* 1 (1971):33–71.

Argues that the function of music is to enhance in some way the quality of individual experience and of human relationships, that music is a metaphorical expression of feeling which can communicate with a detail and truth that language cannot approach, that its methods of communication vary according to its role in social life, and that structures are reflections of patterns of human relations in culture.

39. ———. *Venda Children's Songs: a Study in Ethnomusicology Analysis.* Johannesburg: Witwatersrand University Press, 1967. o.p.

Provides a documentary record of most of the traditional children's songs of the Venda of Northern Transvaal, and an analysis of their music which relates its structure to their cultural background (the Venda classify their songs according to social function). Underlying the analysis is the assumption that music can only be fully understood as humanly organized sound, and that musical styles are therefore based on what man has chosen to select from nature as part of his cultural expression, and not on what nature has imposed on him.

40. Blum, Stephen. "Ethnomusicologists Vis-à-Vis the Fallacies of Contemporary Musical Life." *Pacific Review of Ethnomusicology* 3 (1986):1–19.

Focuses on defining our field of study within the broader contexts of academic and musical life. Pursues a main question/answer point in the education of ethnomusicologists: "we are providing for musical life centered on listening and responsiveness." Particularly singles out for criticism Kerman's remarks about ethnomusicology in *Contemplating Music* (see item

396). "Responses to Blum" follow, pp. 20–41, elicited by *Pacific Review* after a S.E.M. Current Issues Committee presentation, 1985.

41. ———. "Response to the Symposium Papers. Commentary." *Ethnomusicology* 34/3 (Fall 1990):413–21.

As part of a symposium on the Representation of Musical Practice and the Practice of Representation, Blum comments on Turino's suggestion (see item 189) that context is "an ever-expanding series of concentric rings with pathways that cross and connect them," particularly in allowing for temporal as well as spatial dimensions, and joining levels of meaning not represented as concentric rings. Warns against error when the circumstances are not considered (as when people reproduce terms, metaphors, myths, and classifications), as well as errors that come from illusory conceptions of the autonomy of individuals or "cultures" (see Waterman, item 195). Points to another kind of error that makes paradigms and models into fetishes which are endowed with powers mysteriously limiting the human capacity for action. Links arguments of Grenier and Guilbault (item 63) to the latter case, especially when it deflects attention away from the processes of mediation that are part of social life. Concludes that the three papers could have questioned more, particularly the habits we have acquired of reproducing myths about "the West," "Western thought," and "Western music."

42. ———. "Towards a Social History of Musicological Technique." *Ethnomusicology* 19/2 (May 1975):207–231.

Refers mainly to social factors and the comparative study of models in their social contexts. Argues that the scientific and the human aspirations of ethnomusicology require comparative studies to discover or invent appropriate terms of comparison.

43. Bohlman, Philip V. *The Study of Folk Music in the Modern World.* Bloomington: Indiana University Press, 1988.

Argues that most of the changes that folk music undergoes in the modern world can be measured as degrees of modernization and urbanization. To accept the existence of folk music in the modern world requires a reformulation of many of the conservative theories that scholars and ideologues have long used to delimit folk music as a genre. The German folksong "Zum Lauterbach" is used as illustration.

44. Boilès, Charles Lafayette. *Man, Magic, and Musical Occasions.* Ohio: Collegiate Publishing, 1978. o.p.

Attempts to gain a clear understanding of the dynamics of magic in musical behavior. A wide range of magical behavior, with the music and dance that are an intergal part of it, is illustrated. The material is presented according to calendrical rites, life-cycle rites and rituals of conflict.

45. ————. "Tepehua Thought-Song: A Case of Semantic Signaling." *Ethnomusicology* 11/3 (Sept. 1967):267–92.

Describes a special phenomenon of non-verbal communication in which melodies with ascribed meaning are used in a ritual by the Halakiltúnti cult of Tepehua tribe in Northern Veracruz.

46. ————. "Universals of Musical Behavior: a Taxonomic Approach." *World of Music* 26/2 (1984):50–65.

Presents a model of musical behavior. Working from the basic premise that there are no absolute universals of music but that all peoples have some type of musical behavior, the author gives his ordering of categories. Notes that his system has parallels with Seeger's (item 172) and that the two often discussed them together. Boilès' ordering of categories and additional four categories, however, differ from those of Seeger.

47. Chandola, Anoop C. "Some Systems of Musical Scales and Linguistic Principles." *Semiotica* 2 (1970):135–50.

Attempts to demonstrate that musical systems are also semiotic systems, somewhat like language. After explaining the essentials of scale theory in Hindustani raga and discussing briefly a number of relevant linguistic principles, the study focuses on how far linguistic principles can be observed in ragas. Concludes that tonal systems and linguistic systems are governed by almost the same theoretical principles.

48. Chernoff, John M. "The Relevance of Ethnomusicology to Anthropology: Strategies of Inquiry and Interpretation." In *African Musicology: Current Trends*, edited by Jacqueline Cogdell DjeDje and William G. Carter, 59–92. Atlanta: Crossroads Press, 1988.

Reviews Nketia's written work, particularly the concept of "nexus," a means of connection of otherwise discrete institutional realms brought together within the structure of a musical event. Discusses earlier models of cultural analysis, especially the functionalist approach, and subsequent attempts at refinement brought about by symbolic anthropology. Challenges ethnomusicologists to show how an interpretive approach to the institutionalization of music can be applied to anthropology and ethnology. Gives as case study the Dagbamba of Northern Ghana. Calls for future studies that demonstrate the importance of music as a cultural category; also encourages ethnographers to include music within their own research contexts. Considers openness and experimentation essential for future research.

49. Davis, Martha Ellen. "The Social Organization of a Musical Event: The *Fiesta de Cruz* in San Juan, Puerto Rico." *Ethnomusicology* 16/1 (Jan. 1972):38–62.

Describes traditional and contemporary aspects of the *Fiesta de Cruz* and proposes reasons for the fiesta's decline and revival. The success of the revival among the lower class results from adaptation to the functional needs of contemporary society, which are largely recreational.

50. Dowling, W. Jay and Dane L. Harwood. *Music Cognition.* Academic Press series in Cognition and Perception. Orlando: Academic Press, 1986.

A basic textbook on the subject of music cognition, including discussion of the physical properties of sound, the relationships between those properties and the psychological dimensions of what we hear, and finally, of the social contexts of music performance and the importance of cross-cultural studies of musical behavior.

Includes an examination of Lomax's attempt to relate song-style to social-psychological behavior, alternative approaches to music study in cultural context, and examination of cross-cultural universals.

51. Erdely, Stephen. "Ethnic Music in America: An Overview." *Yearbook of the International Music Council* 11 (1979):114–37.

Divides the subject matter into four branches: 1) native, pre-Columbian; 2) that of European settlers; 3) Afro-American; and 4) that of diverse national and ethnic groups. The last is most recent, beginning in the 1880s. Study comprises three phases: recording and gathering; transcription, analysis and classification; and interpretation in light of comparative research. Advocates the collaboration of research team. Provides helpful analysis and classification of the subject for beginners in this area. With sections on: musical types and functions, occasions, and ethnicity.

52. Falck, Robert and Timothy Rice, eds. *Cross-Cultural Perspectives on Music*. Toronto: University of Toronto Press, 1982.

Essays in memory of Mieczyslaw Kolinski from his students, colleagues, and friends are grouped into three broad categories: 1) systematic perspectives, 2) comparative perspectives, and 3) problems and prospects. Includes overview of Kolinski's contributions to the discipline, and list of his works. Notable contributors are Nettl, Boilès, Nattiez, Hopkins, and Merriam. See especially Merriam, "On Objections . . . " (item 107).

53. Feld, Steven. "Aesthetics as Iconicity of Style, or 'Lift-Up-Over-Sounding': Getting into the Kaluli Groove." *Yearbook for Traditional Music* 20/1 (1988):74–113.

Detailed elaboration of the Kaluli notion of *dulugu ganalan* (lift-up-over-sounding) as a style statement (the Kaluli sound). It is found in other Kaluli expressive and interactional modes, as well as being an aesthetic process understood as an iconicity of musical style.

54. ———. "Communication, Speech, and Speech about Music." *Yearbook for Traditional Music* 16 (1984):1–18.

Directs attention to music as a valuable resource for the discovery of musical conceptualization. The phrase "lexical and discourse metaphors" used. Searches for an approach dealing not so much with the logical and philosophical distinctions between speech and music as with the process of meaningful interpretation explicitly conceived as social activity. Points out that speech about music constitutes an interesting source of parallel or exploratory information about metaphoric processes, discourse, interpretive moves, and conceptual ideas or theories about sound.

55. ———. "'Flow Like a Waterfall': The Metaphors of Kaluli Musical Theory." *Yearbook of Traditional Music* 13, 1981 (1982):22–47.

An article inspired by Carl Voegelin's language and culture course where the author was asked to write a paper on the relationships between language and music. He develops two issues in detail: one concerns the nature of verbal representations of musical theory, the other how theoretical thought can be coded in metaphors. He describes how Kaluli systematically metaphorize 'water' and 'sound' to express a theory of form and performance of their vocal music.

56. ———. "Linguistic Models in Ethnomusicology." *Ethnomusicology* 18/2 (May 1974):197–217.

One of the author's earliest expositions on the relationship of language and music. Provides a warning against applying linguistic models to ethnomusicology. Purposely thought-provoking, with useful bibliography. Some ideas had been presented earlier for Merriam's classes in The Arts in Anthropology, 1972–73.

57. ———. *Sound and Sentiment: Birds, Weeping, Poetics and Song in Kaluli Expression*. Publications of the American Folklore Society. New series; vol. 5. Philadelphia: University of Pennsylvania Press, 1982. 2nd ed., 1990.

A significant ethnographic study of sound as a cultural system. The author's analysis of modes and of sound communication leads to an understanding of the ethos and quality of life in Kaluli society. By analyzing the form and performance of weeping, poetics, and song in relation to their origin myth and the bird world they metaphorize, the author reveals Kaluli sound expressions as embodiments of deeply felt sentiments. Neumann reviewed it as "an unusual work . . . it is a major theoretical contribution to ethnomusicology" (*EM* 28:551–4). In a more critical review Nattiez poses methodological questions regarding the study of musical symbolism (*YTM* 15:173–7). The second edition contains a new preface and 31 page postscript including the Kaluli's own reaction to the first edition. As such, this postscript has important implications for the publication of field research.

58. ———. "Sound as a Symbolic System: The Kaluli Drum." In *Explorations in Ethnomusicology: Essays in Honor of David P. McAllester*, ed. by Charlotte Frisbie,147–58. Detroit: Information Coordinators, 1986 (Detroit Monographs in Musicology no. 9). Originally published in *Bikmaus* 4/3 (September 1983):78–89.

Explores the social organization of drumming and its meaning. Contributes an empirical example of how a class of sounds is socially structured to convey meaning. Includes eight metaphoric constructs linking sound and meaning following the Lévi-Strauss model. Raises issues generally relevant to the theory of musical meaning. Shows that while sounds overtly communicate through and about pattern, they may be socially organized to do far more by modulating special categories of sentiment and action when they are brought forth and properly contexted by features of staging and performance.

59. ———. "Sound Structure as Social Structure." *Ethnomusicology* 28/3 (Sept.1984):383–409.

Part of a Symposium on Comparative Sociomusicology together with Roseman (item 154). Includes audience responses. Feld argues that meaningful comparisons are only going to be made from carefully presented examples in their full social context. Addresses two questions: what are the major ways that the classless and generally egalitarian features of one small-scale society reveal themselves in the structure of organized sounds? And, what are the major ways that these same features reveal themselves in the social organization and ideology of soundmakers and soundmaking?

60. Frisbie, Charlotte Johnson. *Kinaaldá A Study of the Navaho Girl's Puberty Ceremony.* Middletown, Conn.: Wesleyan University Press, 1967.

   Aiming to present a detailed account, compares Kinaaldá songs with one another and with other ceremonies' songs to see if they exemplify Navaho chant style, and if their texts are concerned with puberty per se. A final concern is to view it in its cultural context, to see how it expressed the overall value system of the Navaho and how it had been affected by acculturation. Utilizes participant-observer method.

* —— and David P. McAllester, eds. *Navajo Blessingway Singer.* SEE item 114.

61. Giurchescu, Anca. "Power and Charm. Interaction of Adolescent Men and Women in Traditional Settings of Transylvania." *Yearbook for Traditional Music* 18 (1986):37–46.

   Presents research on the people of two villages (Breb and Sirbi) and on the unitary ensemble of their practices in order to discern the meaning of the dance symbol and its function for young men's and women's social interaction, social status differences, and balance of power in the pre-marital stage of life. Although prescribed behavior dominates, dance plays an important role because, among other elements, it takes the dancer "out of himself" and out of everyday life.

62. Gourlay, Kenneth A. "Towards a Reassessment of the Ethnomusicologist's Role in Research," *Ethnomusicology* 22/1 (Jan.1978):1–35.

   Examines the concept of the ethnomusicologist implied in certain theories of research method, investigates the theoretical implications of alternative concepts, and proposes a research model. Discusses Hood, Merriam, Wachsmann, Blacking, Herndon, and S. Blum (he especially reacts to Blum's 1975 article, item 42). Draws on his own experiences with the Karimojong of

Northeastern Uganda, and uses an interactive approach (insider/outsider) from anthropology. See also the author's "Towards a Humanizing Ethnomusicology," *EM* 26 (1982):411–20.

63. Grenier, Line and Jocelyne Guilbault. "'Authority' Revisited: the 'Other' in Anthropology and Popular Music Studies." *Ethnomusicology* 34/3 (Fall 1990):381–97.

Part of a symposium on the Representation of Musical Practice and the Practice of Representation (see also Blum, item 41; Turino, item 189); and Waterman, item 195). Highlights some of the issues raised by the latest findings in anthropology, the alternatives being developed, and their relevance for scholars working on different objects of study. Discusses implications of a central issue in the anthropological "diagnosis" of the current state of ethnography, that of the "Other." Examines studies of popular music in this light and concludes that not everything in recent anthropological arguments need be transferred over, but can be carefully considered. Such arguments can shed new light on already existing debates as well as widen their scope.

64. Harrison, Frank. "Universals in Music: Towards a Methodology of Comparative Research." *World of Music* 19/1–2 (1977):30–6.

Universals are taken to mean elements in common use by all the world's inhabitants, and music as non-linguistic sound when used by human beings. Urges a typology of music-uses and proposes five (with relevant functions), which one writer considers a model (item 110). Concludes that the most striking manifestation of universals in music is music's universality.

65. Harwood, Dane L. "Contributions from Psychology to Musical Universals." *World of Music* 21/1 (1979):48–64.

Reacts to Blacking's statement in *How Musical is Man?* (item 34) that a discussion of human musicality is intrinsically psychological. Suggests what psychology has to offer musicology in contributing to the search for musical universals. Demonstrates why contemporary psychologists are interested in musical behavior, outlines some of the questions faced in looking for "universal" behavior, and hopes to identify a few specific areas of study where psychological theory and method directly address the notion of "universal," particularly in music.

66. ———. "Universals in Music: A Perspective from Cognitive Psychology." *Ethnomusicology* 20/3 (Sept.1976):521–33.

Examines the search for universals in music from the cognitive psychologist's perspective, that is to say, what humans have in common in perceiving, remembering, understanding, and using musical information from their respective cultures. Asserts that all people "construct" their worlds: they impose categories on their perceived environment, and this "categorical perception" is as indicative of musical behavior as it is of vision, language, and in fact, of all human thinking.

*   ——— and W.J. Dowling. *Music Cognition.* SEE Dowling, W. Jay.

67. Helton, Sally Carr. "Markers and Audience Behavior: Relationships Surrounding the Musical Event." IN Discourse in Ethnomusicology II: a Tribute to Alan P. Merriam, edited by Caroline Card et al., 99–130. Bloomington: Indiana University Archives of Traditional Music, 1979.

A marker is defined as any aural, visual, spatial or kinesic phenomenon leading up to or away from the musical performance proper. Seven concerts were analyzed: an opera, an orchestra concert, two jazz concerts, a senior recital, a folk music concert, and a rock 'n' roll concert. The purpose of this study, influenced by Stone's event analysis, was to discover what markers surround a musical performance, the effect they have on audience behavior, and any effect the audience has on them.

68. Henry, Edward O. *Chant the Names of God; Music in Bhojpuri-speaking India.* San Diego, Calif.: San Diego State University Press, 1988.

Expanding on his dissertation topic the author, as an anthropologically trained ethnomusicologist, seeks to establish and examine correlations between social categories and types or styles of music and to compare them with those of surrounding musical cultures. In determining that music is important in the lives of the people who hear and perform it, emphasizes that its study is requisite to a full understanding of the culture.

69. ———. "The Variety of Music in a North Indian Village: Reassessing Cantometrics." *Ethnomusicology* 20/1 (Jan. 1976):49–66.

Uses music and other data gathered in North Indian villages to evaluate conclusions made in *Folk Song Style and Culture* by Lomax about Indian folk music, about the relationship between music and culture in India, and about the relationship between music and culture generally. Concludes that Lomax both exaggerated and de-emphasized different features thus throwing a distorted, if not false, light on village music. Although finding the economic theories of Lomax unacceptable, author feels other aspects merit consideration.

70. Herndon, Marcia. "The Cherokee Ballgame Cycle: An Ethnomusicologist's View." *Ethnomusicology* 15/3 (Sept. 1971): 339–52.

Although originally interested in comparing different approaches (see Fogelson, item 364), the two authors discovered almost identical methods and goals. The ballgame cycle is identified as a cultural performance or occasion. Using a cognitive analysis, the author concludes that: 1) since it often accompanies *rites de passage*, the occasion may yield information about basic functions of music in human cognitive systems; and 2) the occasion may provide both the key to and confirmation of basic values and beliefs in a given society.

71. ———. "Toward Evaluating Musical Change Through Musical Potential." *Ethnomusicology* 31/3 (Fall 1987):455–68.

Result of a seminar on Musical Retention and Change (1986) and later an S.E.M. paper (1986). Acknowledges that these proposals are tentative: that a combination of several previous ideas and approaches to musical change constitutes, with one addition, a framework for constructing rough topographies of the potential of musical systems for change. Topographies are felt to provide a basis for diachronic and cross-cultural musical comparison, while allowing maximum freedom in description and analysis. Reviews events in musical change that have influenced the proposed framework. Concepts of equilibrium, process, and potential are introduced. Assumes that focus of research on musical change should be internal (not external) although external factors and events may inform (but not direct) the analysis. Illustrates with field data from Malta and from Eastern Cherokee Indians of southeastern U.S.

72. ———— and Roger Brunyate, eds. *Proceedings of a Symposium on Form in Performance, Hard-Core Ethnography.* Austin: Office of the College of Fine Arts, University of Texas, 1975.

Marks the beginning of adaptation from the discipline of folklore and its studies in the ethnography of performance into ethnomusicology performance theory. Based on folklore work by Roger Abrahams and Richard Bauman, who contributed "The Theoretical Boundaries of Performance." Most papers are of an informal nature meant to be heard rather than read. Includes discussions which are sometimes more stimulating than the papers.

73. ———— and Norma McLeod. *Music as Culture.* Darby, Pa.: Norwood Editions, 1980; 2nd ed., 1981; reprinted 1986.

Authors stress two assumptions: music exists *as* culture rather than *in* culture; and it is *performed*. The revised 1981 edition incorporated criticisms of the earlier edition including developments in theory, practice and focus. Criticized by Rice as retreating from asking *why* people make music to asking *how* (*EM* 31/3:484).

74. Hood, Mantle. "The Challenge of Bi-Musicality." *Ethnomusicology* 4/2 (1960):55–9.

For the first time the author presents his thesis that a Western student of ethnomusicology can become fluent in playing the music of several different musical cultures and thereby become bi-musical, tri-musical or quadri-musical.

* SEE ALSO ———. *The Ethnomusicologist.* (item 6)

75. ———. "Ethnomusicology." In *Harvard Dictionary of Music*, 298–300. 2nd ed. Cambridge: Belknap Press of Harvard University Press, 1969.

Concerns the definition of ethnomusicology as "an approach to the study of any music, not only in terms of itself but also in relation to its cultural context." Compare definitions of Merriam and Kolinski.

———. "Music, the Unknown." SEE Harrison, Frank Ll. et al., *Musicology* (item 381).

76. Hopkins, Pandora. "Aural Thinking." In *Cross-Cultural Perspectives on Music*, edited by Robert Falck and Timothy Rice, 143–61. Toronto: University of Toronto Press, 1982.

Treats an experiment in the cross-cultural perception of a rhythmic pattern in Norwegian fiddling. One of the few studies of music conceptualization in Western folk traditions. The research and paper became part of her Ph.D. dissertation, University of Pennsylvania, 1978, and was expanded in her book, *Aural Thinking* (item 77).

77. ———. *Aural Thinking in Norway: Performance and Communication with the Hardingfele.* New York: Human Sciences Press, 1986.

Aural thinking is originally a concept of Rudolf Arnheim and concerns the cognitive nature of musical communication. Demonstrates the importance of intentionality as a determining factor in the occurrence (or non-occurrence) or change in music. Study was founded on three assumptions: 1) that all traditions have histories, 2) that all musical systems are meaningful (in a musical sense), and 3) that theories must be generated from the insights of the *spelemenn* themselves. Focus on informants' musical cognition. With bibliography (pp. 291–307).

78. ———. "The Homology of Music and Myth: Views of Lévi-Strauss on Musical Structure." *Ethnomusicology* 21/2 (May 1977):247–61.

Reaction to Lévi-Strauss' utilization of structural concepts in European art music as the intellectual framework for his major work on mythology (1964–71). Author concludes that, despite some problems, his concepts are liberating and free the scholar from making assumptions that have never been proved but have been difficult to avoid. Feels these concepts should lend themselves fruitfully to further permutations and transformations.

79. Kaemmer, John E. "Between the Event and the Tradition: A New Look at Music in Sociocultural Systems." *Ethnomusicology* 24/1 (Jan. 1980):61–74.

Draws attention to a level of analysis that lies between the musical event and the localized musical tradition. Suggests a typology of musical events that might serve as a conceptual tool for research into the relationships between musical forms and the forms of society in which they are produced. Defines five different types of music complex: individualistic, communal, contractual, sponsored, and commercial.

80. Kaeppler, Adrienne. "Aesthetics of Tongan Dance." *Ethnomusicology* 15/2 (May 1971):175–85.

Concerns the realm of musical conceptualization amenable to oral-verbal analysis. Through broadening the definition of aesthetics to be used cross-culturally and defining art to encompass what non-Western as well as Western societies perceive to be art, author attempts to illuminate the nature of aesthetic judgments and experiences in non-Western culture. Among the Tongans, she concludes, there is a verbalized aesthetic pertaining to structure, performance and emotional states. These must be looked at, however, through the eyes of the people under investigation.

81. *Karawitan: Source Readings in Javanese Gamelan and Vocal Music.* Edited by Judith Becker and Alan H. Feinstein. 3 vols. Michigan Papers on South and Southeast Asia, nos. 23, 30, and 31.

Ann Arbor: University of Michigan Center for South and Southeast Asian Studies, 1984, 1987, and 1988.

Collection of writings on Javanese music by Javanese authors, translated into English. Provides a service for Javanese musical traditions as well as for music theory and history from an indigenous perspective. Instructive preliminary essay describes the problem of meaning that confronts the translator as well as the contextual problems inherent in translation. Explanation of calendrical systems, chronograms and court rankings of musicians is helpful. Writings cover period from 1926 to early 1970s. Includes four useful appendices, glossary of Javanese terms, extensive collection of notation, biographies of the authors, and bibliography of sources mentioned in the texts or referred to by the translator. Brinner's review (*EM* 34:140–6) notes that this series offers a model for its kind (works in other musical traditions with significant indigenous writing).

82.   Kartomi, Margaret J. "The Processes and Results of Musical Culture Contact: A Discussion of Terminology and Concepts." *Ethnomusicology* 25/2 (May 1981):227–49.

Discusses transculturation between non-Western and Western cultures, particularly the case of Portuguese-derived *kroncong* genre of Indonesia.

83.   Keeling, Richard, ed. *Women in North American Indian Music: Six Essays*. Special Series No. 6. Bloomington: Society for Ethnomusicology, 1989.

Three men and three women offer some substantive explanations concerning the apparent male dominance in music making among the Shoshone, Ojibway, Navajo, Gros Ventre, sub-Arctic Algonkian, and Yurok peoples. Keeling's introduction gives a brief historical survey of music and gender and summarizes the focus of each paper. His epilogue asks for new fieldwork aimed at answering gender-related questions and critical research in existing sources. Essays grew out of a panel discussion entitled "Gender as a Determinant of Style in American Indian Music" at the 1987 S.E.M. Annual Meeting.

84. Keil, Charles. "Participatory Discrepancies and the Power of Music." *Cultural Anthropology* 2/3 (August 1987):275–83.

Outlines how an alternative musicology of participatory discrepancies might proceed. Uses the concept of participation as defined by Lévy-Bruhl and refined by Owen Barfield. Feels the need for more participatory consciousness if we are to get back into ecological synchrony with ourselves and with the natural world.

85. ———. *Tiv Song; the Sociology of Art in a Classless Society.* Chicago: University of Chicago Press, 1979.

A very personal, perceptive and unique account of a field experience and the philosophical position resulting from it. Incorporating the interactive approach of insider/outsider, the author develops a Marxist perspective in his ethnological approach to music and the arts in Tiv society. Gourlay remarks that the book is perhaps less important for the answers it gives than for the questions it raises (*EM* 24/1:119–23). Work won the Chicago Folklore Prize in 1980.

86. ——— and Angeliki Keil. "Musical Meaning: A Preliminary Report." *Ethnomusicology* 10/2 (May 1966):153–73.

Concerned with the coordinates between music and culture. Uses Charles Osgood's "semantic differential" instrument and gives respondent results (profiles) in interpreting seven musical experiences: four Ravi Shankar selections, a Bach two part invention played by Landowska, a B.B. King urban blues work, and a John Coltrane Quintet jazz piece.

87. Kingsbury, Henry. *Music, Talent and Performance: A Conservatory Cultural System.* Philadelphia: Temple University Press, 1988.

Taking as his "field" the American conservatory of music, author offers an innovative anthropological analysis of the Western notion of "talent" and compares its cultural character with the fact that many non-Western societies have no such concept. Critically reviewed by Koskoff (*EM* 34:311–15), who cites "A Song in a

Strange Land" as the strongest chapter because it examines the "cult of the individual" as symbolically represented in the ritual of the solo recital. Included is a discussion of stage fright, a physical response to the inability of the performer to see him/herself maintaining an "aesthetic illusion." A book worth reading, but the author possibly goes too far to show the conservatory in a negative light, thereby undermining his objectivity.

88. Kippen, James. *The Tabla of Lucknow; a Cultural Analysis of a Musical Tradition.* Cambridge: Cambridge University Press, 1988.

Shows that the individuality of the Lucknow tradition is linked to the individuality of the cultural climate that sustained it through most of the late 18th and 19th centuries. Believes that the disappearance of that climate along with the demise of princely patronage and the increased control of the State during the 20th century, have contributed to Lucknow's position as a cultural backwater where the older traditions struggle to survive alongside new ones that cater to the tastes of modern Indian audiences. Participant observation used in research.

89. Koskoff, Ellen. "The Music Network." *Ethnomusicology* 26/3 (Sept. 1982):353–70.

Organizes concepts of musical cognition into clusters of categories with which an informant associates. Her results demonstrate the richness of individuals' musical conceptualization that "ordinary language alone cannot exhaust." They also emphasize the degree to which individuals may vary in their conceptualization of music and the extensive meshing of these concepts with ideas drawn from other realms of experience. Questionnaire is included as an appendix (pp. 369–70).

90. List, George. "The Boundaries of Speech and Song." In *Readings in Ethnomusicology*, edited by David P. McAllester, 253–68. New York: Johnson Reprint Corp., 1971. [First published in *Ethnomusicology* 7/1 (Jan. 1963):1–16.]

Addresses the development of a method of classification in order to clarify the distinctions between speech and song. Author proposes a chart, Figure 9, which is analogous to a hemispheric map of the world.

91. ———. "Ethnomusicology: a Discipline Defined." *Ethnomusicology* 23/1 (Jan. 1979):1–4.

Revised version of a statement made at a colloquium on future directions in ethnomusicology, 1977. Argues that ethnomusicology can only be defined by considering what the ethnomusicologist is better equipped to accomplish than others involved in activity related to music, and concludes that it has become a discipline in its own right. The author's definition: the study of humanly produced patterns of sound, sound patterns that the members of the culture who produce them or the scholar who studies them conceive to be music. The ethnomusicologist differs from the historical musicologist in the focus upon the performance of the music, whether or not it is notated.

92. ———. "On the Non-Universality of Musical Perspectives." *Ethnomusicology* 15/3 (Sept. 1971):399–402.

A rebuttal to ideas presented at a S.E.M. panel, Universal Perspectives of Music, 1970 (see also McAllester, item 97; Wachsmann, item 194; and Seeger, item 168). Stands opposed to McAllester but reinforces Wachsmann's position. Feels that the most universal characteristic of music is its non-universality as a means of communication: it communicates to members of the in-group only, whoever they may be. Also cites the definition that what music communicates cannot be expressed in words. Doubts that there is a universal response to music. The single universal aspect of music is that most people make it.

93. Lomax, Alan. *Cantometrics: an Approach to the Anthropology of Music.* Berkeley: University of California Extension Media Center, 1976. 7 cassette tapes title: *Cantometrics: a Method in Musical Anthropology.*

A condensed and revised update of Lomax's *Cantometrics* project, often used as a basic textbook. With the cassette tapes it is possible to hear the cross-cultural comparisons in the music. Reviewed positively by David Locke (*EM* 25:527–9) who notes that the cassette tapes are the heart of the publication. Jeff Titon substantially agrees (*JAF* 95/377:370–4).

94. ———. *Folk Song Style and Culture*. American Association for the Advancement of Science, Publication No. 88. Washington, D.C.: American Association for the Advancement of Science, 1968; reprinted New Brunswick, N.J.: Transaction Pubs., 1978.

The result of extensive research, applies the thesis that song style symbolizes and reinforces certain important aspects of social structure in all cultures. Termed the Cantometrics Project, it admits a behavioral bias and a limitation mainly to song. Chapters explain the method, the experiment, the coding, as well as song as a measurement of culture. Hewitt Pantaleoni's review (*YIFMC* 4:158–61) severely criticizes Lomax's cultural bias (see also item 102).

95. McAllester, David P. "The First Snake Song." In *Theory and Practice: Essays Presented to Gene Weltfish*, edited by Stanley Diamond, 1–27. The Hague: Mouton, 1980.

Shows how the analysis of a song together with the song text may reveal some of the categories of thought, the cognitive matrix, from which the snake song arises. Placed in the sequential context of seven other songs, in the whole ceremony, and in the myth of the Shootingway, one of the most important of the long and complex Navajo ceremonials.

96. ———. *Readings in Ethnomusicology*. Middletown: Wesleyan University Press; New York: Johnson Reprint, 1971. [o.p.]

Attempts to present characteristic examples of various kinds and levels of writing by reprinting them in one volume. Many are pre-1960. Division by sub-sections: The Field (Nettl), Notation and Classification (Reinhard, C. Seeger, Hood, Freeman and Merriam, Bayard), History (Collaer, Herzog, Rhodes, Grame, Nettl), Functionalism (R. Waterman, Burrows, Conklin and Maceda, McAllester, Lomax, List, Meyer, Nadel), and Regional Studies (R. Brown, Nketia, Picken, Malm).

97. ———. "Some Thoughts on 'Universals' in World Music." *Ethnomusicology* 15/3 (Sept. 1971):379–80.

From the S.E.M. session on universals, 1970 (see also List, item 92; Wachsmann, item 194; and Seeger, item 168). Remarks that scholars stress differences among musics and that maybe it is time to look at similarities. Qualifies the fact that there are probably no absolute universals in music because of human variability and complexity. Feels there are lots of near-universals, such as sense of tonal center in establishing a tendency for going somewhere, and some kind of development and form. Author is particularly interested in what music does to people.

98. McLean, Mervyn. "Song Loss and Social Context Among the New Zealand Maori." *Ethnomusicology* 9/3 (Sept. 1965):296–304.

Examines the mechanism by which social change among the Maori may affect the transmission of traditional chant. This in light of the fact that they have a strong resistance to change but a decline in language ability. Progressive influences that become more important are superstitious restrictions on performance, decline of memorizing ability due to increasing literacy, and fewer opportunities for incidental learning. Later when pool of singers diminishes, attempts to keep songs within particular families or tribes hastens the process. The last phase comes as the group singing in an area breaks down. Believes the situation is not hopeless; the process can be arrested at any one of the above levels. Concludes that social changes are the most important determinant of song loss, especially loss of function.

99. ———. "Towards the Differentiation of Music Areas in Oceania." *Anthropos* 74 (1979):717–36.

Uses hand clustering methods and a limited sample of around forty areas and forty traits to differentiate five music areas for Oceania. Presents interim results of a long-term project which seeks to differentiate music areas in Oceania. Information was obtained from three sources: 1) printed literature (travel, missionary as well as music titles); 2) analysis of published transcriptions; and 3) auditing of field tapes (University of Auckland).

100. McLeod, Norma, and Marcia Herndon, eds. *Ethnography of Musical Performance.* Norwood, Pa.: Norwood Editions, 1980.

Contains eight articles that reflect the application of ethnology of communication to the study of music. Articles are of uneven quality, but those of Frisbie, Seeger, Shield, and Herndon and McLeod are recommended. The last, titled "The Interrelationship of Style and Occasion in the Maltese *Spirtu Pront,*" suggests a method by which native categories may be integrated with those of the ethnomusicologist.

101. Manuel, Peter. *Popular Musics of the Non-Western World.* New York: Oxford University Press, 1988.

Aims to contribute to the understanding and appreciation of non-Western popular genres by describing them in a manner at once readable and informative to the specialist. These are forms and genres that have grown up to replace traditional musical styles in some parts of the world. Introductory chapter on perspectives, subsequent chapters by broad culture areas. A good introductory study, but not exhaustive. Useful 8–page bibliography as well as glossary. Positively reviewed by David Coplan (*EM* 34:151–4) and by Krister Malm (*YTM* 22:146–7). Malm remarks, however, that it can only serve as an introduction because information about less well-known popular musics is not included. Won the ASCAP-Deems Taylor Award in 1990.

102. Maranda, Elli Köngas. "Deep Significance and Surface Significance: Is Cantometrics Possible?" *Semiotica* 2 (1970):173–84.

A highly critical review article discussing Lomax's *Folk Song Style and Culture* (item 94). Calls Cantometrics a sort of paramusicology, cites incompatibilities in Lomax's statements, lack of documentation to support generalizations, his avoidance of findings that do not fit the formulas put forth. Remarks on imbalance in the sampling of songs, and on frequent unmeasurables or subjective impressions. Nevertheless, finds the analysis of song style to be distinctive and interesting; also that Lomax has discovered a mechanism by which deep significance can be translated systematically into surface significance.

*   SEE ALSO Merriam, Alan. *Anthropology of Music* (item 11).

103. ————. "Definitions of 'Comparative Musicology' and 'Ethnomusicology': An Historical-Theoretical Perspective." *Ethnomusicology* 21 (May 1977):189–204.

A discussion of the history of the two terms and the consequences of the change from one to the other within the limits of the American experience. Author is somewhat biased towards defining what ethnomusicology ought to be. Appendix contains references and quoted definitions by various researchers in chronological order.

104. ————. *Ethnomusicology of the Flathead Indians*. Chicago: Aldine Press, 1967.

One of the first "modern" studies on a particular Indian group that the author had studied in the early 50s. Coverage is broad and thorough, and includes the transcription and analysis of 226 songs using statistical analysis of the melodies. Reviewed by Rhodes (*YIFMC* 1:241–5) and in review essays by William K. Powers and Mieczyslaw Kolinski (*EM* 14/1:67–99).

105. ————. "Ethnomusicology Revisited." *Ethnomusicology* 13/2 (May 1969):213–29.

The first of two lectures given at U.C.L.A. in 1968, in which he attempts to generalize as to why particular groups of scholars concentrate their efforts in particular directions. Quotes from an earlier and already then rather outdated (1946) *Harvard Dictionary*, and from *Musicology* by Harrison, Palisca and Hood, in a general attack on musicology. Dissects the discipline of anthropology into four parts. Most of the article consists of his ideas about the differences between the two approaches. Author reiterates his model based on three analytic levels: conceptualizations about music, behavior in relation to music, and music sound itself; and tries to bring the two parts of the discipline closer together.

106. ————. "Ethnomusicology Today." *Current Musicology* 20 (1975):50–66.

Continues, after a six year break, his "revisited" remarks. Feels, however, as if the current state of flux is not as simple and clearcut as he thought. Frets over some groups of people who call themselves ethnomusicologists but who are really simply just performers of ethnic music, music educators, those who see music including Western "classical" in a global context (including composers), and others of a heterogenous sort with a variety of interests (e.g., music therapists). In summary he gives an idea of what ethnomusicology is doing, and from that an overview of what is going on in the anthropological "camp." Sees a move towards music sound structure through a concern with music as a socio-cultural phenomenon, and presently towards a preoccupation with musical emotion, feeling and meaning.

107. ———. "On Objections to Comparison in Ethnomusicology." In *Cross-Cultural Perspectives in Music*, edited by Robert Falck and Timothy Rice, 174–89. Toronto: Univ. of Toronto Press, 1982.

One of the last contributions before his untimely death. Reviews past and present objectives and finds them all wanting in one way or the other. Argues that although comparison is not the only legitimate goal of ethnomusicology, scholars must seek to make it a usable tool rather than abandon it altogether.

108. ———. "Purposes of Ethnomusicology: an Anthropological View." *Ethnomusicology* 7 (1963):206–13 [Reprinted in slightly abridged form in *Every Man His Way, Readings in Cultural Anthropology*, edited by Alan Dundes, 343–52. Englewood Cliffs: Prentice-Hall, 1968.]

Remarks made at a Plenary Session of the 1962 S.E.M. annual meeting, when ethnomusicologists discussed basic problems in their field. Author hopes that dialogue will lead toward a better understanding of each other's point of view, and, more important, to a conscious shaping of what ethnomusicology is, does, and should be.

109. Meyer, Leonard B. "Universalism and Relativism in the Study of Ethnic Music." *Ethnomusicology* 4 (1960):49–54.

Poses questions that might lead to a more fruitful and enlightened analysis of the nature of value in Western as well as non-Western music, and at the same time help to clarify the correlative problem of universality vs. relativity of values. Some of this was already discussed in his *Emotion and Meaning in Music* (1956).

110. Modir, Hafez. "Research Models in Ethnomusicology Applied to the *Radif* Phenomenon in Iranian Classical Music." *Pacific Review of Ethnomusicology* 3 (1986):63–78.

Contains a list of "Models in Ethnomusicology," pp. 68–72. Includes a figure containing the collective examination of nine models that reveals both continuity and contradiction: Meyer, C. Seeger, Merriam, Blacking, Harrison, Harwood, Rahn, Boilès, and Nketia.

111. Mueller, John H. "A Sociological Approach to Musical Behavior." *Ethnomusicology* 7/3 (Sept. 1963):216–20.

Author, as a sociologist, comments on Merriam's article in the same issue, "Purposes of Ethnomusicology." Proposes that music is inter-human and interpersonal behavior.

112. Nattiez, Jean-Jacques. "Comparisons within a Culture: the Examples of the Katajjag of the Inuit." In *Cross-Cultural Perspectives on Music*, edited by Robert Falck and Timothy Rice, 134–40. Toronto: University of Toronto Press, 1982.

Proposes an analytical grid, inspired by certain concepts of musical semiotics, to explain the discrepancies within a given musical genre by establishing a link between contradictory information and different groups. Contains an example of a theoretical map with historical density. Helpful to the study and description of musical styles as an initial attempt to reconstruct history.

113. ———. "Some Aspects of Inuit Vocal Games." *Ethnomusicology* 27/3 (Sept. 1983):457–75.

Presents already accessible data about Inuit vocal game genre and some methodological reflections inspired by the Montreal Semiotics group research. Sections discuss distribution and terminology, ethnographic meaning, stylistic analysis, compositional processes, and cultural explanation. Nattiez concludes that the task of musical semiotics is not to reduce the phenomena it studies to universal and global explanations, but to describe the specificity of forms present in a culture and grasp the nature of the relations existing among them.

114. *Navajo Blessingway Singer: The Autobiography of Frank Mitchell, 1881–1967.* Edited by Charlotte J. Frisbie and David P. McAllester. Tucson: University of Arizona Press, 1978, 1980.

Excellent example of an "oral autobiography" and the result of 18 years' archival/library research as well as interviews. Introduction describes Mitchell briefly in the context of his religion and culture, the span of the fieldwork, the human relations in the fieldwork, methods of fieldwork, editing procedure, and analysis. Analytic discussion, however, is minimal.

115. Nettl, Bruno, ed. *Eight Urban Musical Cultures: Tradition and Change.* Urbana: University of Illinois Press, 1978.

Collection of essays that demonstrate different approaches, musical and anthropological, to the problem of determining the direction of traditional music in a modernized or urban setting. Nettl's introduction surveys urban ethnomusicology's history, its theoretical framework, reasons for its uneven development, and importance to future research. Other contributions by Blum, Coplan, the L'Armands, Neuman, Riddle, Stigberg, and Ware.

116. ———. "Mozart and the Ethnomusicological Study of Western Culture: an Essay in Four Movements." *Yearbook for Traditional Music* 21 (1989):1–16.

Underscores the need for ethnomusicologists to include, with all the "exotic" music they study, that of European and American concert traditions. Intended as food for thought, and a view from a different perspective, but also by implication as a critique of ethnomusicological approaches. Examines the principles and values underlying Western music and sees concepts like genius, discipline, efficiency, the hierarchical pyramid of musics and composers, the musician as stranger and outsider, the wonders of complexity, the stimulus of innovation, and music having the possibility of metaphorical extensions. Also mentions negative elements.

117. ———. "Musical Areas Reconsidered: A Critique of North American Indian Research." In *Essays in Musicology in Honor of Dragan Plamenac on his 70th Birthday*, edited by Gustav Reese and Robert J. Snow, 181–89. New York: DaCapo Press, 1977. [Originally published by Pittsburgh: University of Pittsburgh Press, 1969, pp.181–89.]

A postscript and revision to his *North American Indian Musical Styles* (Philadelphia, 1954). Defines his task as trying to show what modifications are indicated in the scheme of musical areas in North America with which he began working over ten years ago. Revisions include making five areas instead of the original six. Retracts his earlier steps now that more data are available; the result is, however, that the areas are less clear.

118. ———. "Non-Western and Folk Music, and Ethnomusicology." *Musical Quarterly* 68/2 (April 1982):153–60.

A critique of the *New Grove Dictionary of Music & Musicians*. Comments on the inclusion of a large amount of material on non-Western and folk music, and on related matters of theory and methodology. He criticizes the somewhat uneven quality of coverage (between different African nations, for example), the chronological ordering of the bibliographies, the unevenness of long articles dealing with fundamental concepts or major divisions of a field of knowledge, and lack of intercultural perspective in articles dealing with fundamental issues in musical thought. He particularly praises Powers' "Mode" article, other articles on Asian music, Cohen's "Melographs," etc.

119. ———. *Reference Materials in Ethnomusicology; a Bibliographic Essay on Primitive, Oriental and Folk Music*. Detroit Studies in

Music Bibliography, 1. 2nd ed. rev. Detroit: Information Coordinators, 1973.

In narrative form, this is one of the few reference works after 1960 directed towards librarians and students in order to help them find and evaluate general information. Sections include: preface, introduction, definitions, surveys, techniques of research, elements of music, instruments, special approaches, collections, periodicals, directories, and bibliographies. Author reminds us that the field of ethnomusicology has been emerging, since 1950, as a discipline requiring special treatment in education, in the publishing world, in libraries. The bibliography itself is only a small part of the total work.

* SEE ALSO ———. *The Study of Ethnomusicology; Twenty-Nine Issues and Concepts* (item 16).

120. ———. "A Technique of Ethnomusicology Applied to Western Culture." *Ethnomusicology* 7/3 (Sept. 1963):221–24.

Comments on Merriam's "Purposes of Ethnomusicology" article. Concludes that the study of music classifications by people in a particular cultural group should tell us something about the culture and the music. Further that the development of such a technique for non-Western music—and its subsequent application in Western music—indicates the importance of ethnomusicological methods for the study of all musical culture.

121. ———. *Theory and Method in Ethnomusicology.* New York: Free Press of Glencoe, 1964.

A standard work published in the same year as Merriam's "classic" on anthropological method (item 11). Describes the discipline and provides some theoretical background for the beginner. Chapter 2, "Bibliographic Resources of Ethnomusicology," reviews the important literature up to 1964.

122. ———. *The Western Impact on World Music; Change, Adaptation, and Survival.* New York: Schirmer, 1985.

A series of short essays intended to supply the reader with samples of the complexities of musical change. Written in a conversational style, it could be used in special cases as an introductory textbook for the questions it raises. Thorough reviews by Qureshi (*EM* 30/3:574–8) and Kartomi (*YTM* 19:117–20).

123. ———. "Western Musical Values and the Character of Ethnomusicology." *World of Music* 24/1 [sic] (1984):29–42.

Concludes that, whether it was good or not, we accept the fact that ethnomusicology grew up under the aegis of Western classical music. It is here that we look for the ways the discipline first developed and for the roots of some of the methods and approaches. Attempts to ferret out some of the values of our musical culture, particularly as expressed before and after 1900, and to see how they affected the development of ethnomusicology.

124. Neuman, Daniel M. *The Life of Music in North India: The Organization of an Artistic Tradition.* Detroit: Wayne State University Press; New Delhi: Manohar, 1980.

Anthropological study of Hindustani music culture based mainly on conversations with vocalists and instrumentalists in Delhi. Expands on his doctoral dissertation (1974). Principally concerns the kinds of groups performers say they belong to. Helpful for event analysis. Reviewed by Deborah Hayes with minor criticisms about the editing (*EM* 25/2:338–9).

125. ———. "The Social Organization of a Music Tradition: Hereditary Specialists in North India." *Ethnomusicology* 21/2 (May 1979):233–45.

Explores the principles upon which North Indian art music is socially organized as well as looking at the relationship between patterns of human organization and the patterns of sound produced as a result of human interaction. Believes that musical specialists can reveal some of the processes by which a music responds to its more general environment.

126. Nketia, J. H. Kwabena. "The Aesthetic Dimension in Ethnomusicological Studies." *World of Music* 26/1 [sic] (1984):3–28.

A good survey article about aesthetics. Considers its study to be an extension of ethnomusicological investigation into different aspects of music and its socio-cultural context. Aesthetics goes beyond analysis of the use and function of music in culture, or its interpretation in terms of cultural themes and causal relations to the basis of its interpretation, evaluation and appreciation on the experimental level. Believes it is not possible to relate fully to a musical culture on its own terms (as opposed to the terms of one's background) until one is thoroughly familiar with its aesthetic principles.

127. ———. "Contextual Strategies of Inquiry and Systematization." *Ethnomusicology* 34/1 (Winter 1990):75–97.

Emphasizes the contexts of music-making. Reiterates the author's personal view that ethnomusicology is a discipline that combines formal and contextual techniques in the scholarly study of music. Contextual technique is shown to be integrative, combining both analysis and synthesis at every step in the systematization process (The Seeger Lecture, 1989).

128. ———. "Integrating Objectivity and Experience in Ethnomusicological Studies." *World of Music* 27/3 (1985):3–19.

Struggles with the problem of defining the field. He complains that current approaches in ethnomusicology tend to be monistic or characterized by one dimension of music. Asks for the development of an integrative technique that enables the scholar to group and regroup his data; and for methods of synthesis that bring together the different aspects of music and music making in a meaningful and coherent manner. Rice chides Nketia for failing to give answers about how this can be brought about, and worse, suggesting that it is precisely this sort of methodological classification (as culture, as object of aesthetic interest and as language) that may have to be overcome or altered (see item 148).

129. ———. "The Juncture of the Social and the Musical: The Methodology of Cultural Analysis." *World of Music* 23/2 (1981):22–31.

An earlier attempt at definition. Critical of a shift of emphasis from musical experience to the behavior that surrounds music, and the assumption that there is a one-to-one correspondence and a relationship of causality between aspects of music and aspects of culture and society.

130. ———. "The Problem of Meaning in African Music." *Ethnomusicology* 6/1 (1962):1–7.

Advocates an integrated approach (musicological and anthropological) to the study of meaning in music (African music in particular). Outlines a contextual technique which enables the various modes of meaning in African music to be investigated and studied in a comprehensive manner without losing sight of "music in culture" or of our ultimate task of contributing to the study of man "what can be known of man as music maker and music user."

131. ———. "Universal Perspectives in Ethnomusicology." *World of Music* 26/2 (1984):3–24.

Suggests three approaches to the study of universals: 1) from the creative perspective (in terms of materials and processes capable of application or use outside their original environment), 2) from the empirical perspective (in terms of common properties of musical systems and their distribution as well as the basis of their cross-cultural differentiation), and 3) from the perspective of comparative functionalism (it searches for the extrinsic basis of universals). Some consider Nketia's six universal typologies a research model of music in culture (item 110).

132. Porter, James. "Ballad Explanations, Ballad Reality, and the Singer's Epistemics." *Western Folklore* 45 (1986):110–25.

Argues for attention to the complex ways in which singers confer meaning on their songs (in the general sphere of performer's worldview and its actualization in performance). Introduces the term *epistemics* to the study of traditional singing. Refers to the function that the singer perceives a song to have within the performance context as well as to the complex of meanings the singer brings to the song. Urges the scholar not to bypass the complex attitudes and notions that singers hold towards the songs they sing.

133. ———. "Context, Epistemics and Value: A Conceptual Performance Model Reconsidered." *Selected Reports* 7 (1988):69–97.

Referring to his 1976 article on Jeannie Robertson he proposes a rethinking and suggests modifications. Stresses importance of studying stylistic change.

134. ———. "Jeannie Robertson's 'My Son David': A Conceptual Performance Model." *Journal of American Folklore* 89/351 (Jan.-Feb.1976):7–26.

A conceptual performance model that concentrates on the concept of the identity of a single song sung under a variety of conditions and over a period of time by the same singer. The completed model is an empirical one. Porter later wrote (item 133) that he wanted to find the meaning of the song from the singer's point of view.

135. ———. "Prolegomena to a Comparative Study of European Folk Music." *Ethnomusicology* 21/3 (Sept. 1977):435–51.

Attempts to clarify some of the major issues involved in a comparative study of the folk music of Europe, and to draw together the threads of argument in relation to each of the problems. Suggests elaborating a model related to multidimensional typologies of the major style areas. Together, typologies of major European style regions can form a basis for elaborating this model. Argues for a mechanical model over a statistical one.

136. ——— and A. Jihad Racy. "'Introduction' to Issues in the Conceptualization of Music." *Selected Reports* 7 (1988):vii-xvii.

Defines musical conceptualization as the overall scheme of musical cognition and creation. Study of performer's or informant's conceptualizations is a primary concern. Speech about music (analysis of language) is most often used to discover informant's conceptualization. Essays address the question of how musical conceptualization operates in diverse frameworks. Diversity of factors include: dynamics of socializing, researcher's own pattern of musical cognition, individual cognitive strategies, cognitive transformation within the individual, musician's articulate world-view, musico-religious conceptualization in traditional and innovative communities, and systems of social and musical interaction in a recent historical context.

137. Powers, Harold. "First Meeting of the ICTM Study Group on Maqam." *Yearbook for Traditional Music* 20/1 (1988):199–218.

An outgrowth of Jürgen Elsner's work (and indirectly of Powers' *New Grove* "Mode" contribution), the group covered a broad range of areas and topics, and its meetings involved four main types of presentation: 1) cross-regional essays, 2) regional traditions within the maqam world, 3) traditions tangentially connectable with maqam or maqam-related traditions, and 4) folk music practices outside such traditions but thought to have some analogous features. All papers are succinctly summarized and enlightening conclusions offered.

138. ———. "Mode." In *The New Grove Dictionary of Music and Musicians* 12 (1980):376–450.

Comprehensive examination of what constitutes mode in both Western and non-Western musics. Treatment is broad and discusses the term as a concept of both scale type and melody type. Covers medieval theory, polyphonic modal theory, modal scales and folksong. Maqam, raga, patet, and choshi are analyzed as an expansion and internationalization of the concept.

139. Qureshi, Regula. "Qawwali: Making the Music Happen in the Sufi Assembly." In *Performing Arts in India*, ed. by Bonnie C. Wade, 118–57. Lanham, Md.: University Press of America, 1983. Reprinted in *Asian Music* 18/2 (1987).

Takes as its starting point the assumption that music is part of culture and therefore linked to its socio-cultural context. The author establishes musical structure through the conceptualizations of musicians and musical theorists, and sets up the conceptual framework of a musical performance in order to arrive at a contextual analysis of music in performance.

140. ———. *Sufi Music of India and Pakistan: Sound, Context, and Meaning in Qawwali*. Cambridge Studies in Ethnomusicology. Cambridge: Cambridge University Press, 1986.

The author's purpose is to comprehend how music communicates to those who listen to it, how they in turn affect the performance, and thus to discover the underlying meaning. Within recent ethnomusicological writing the approach falls within performance studies, but differs in that its primary focus is on the musical sound idiom. This approach has hitherto been used only for art music traditions. Manuel's review praises the book's ethnographic value and methodological originality (*YTM* 21:131).

141. Racy, Jihad. "Sound and Society, the *Takht* Music of Early Twentieth Century Cairo." *Selected Reports* 7 (1988):139–70.

Attempts to understand the connections between professional music-makers as a social group and the music they perform. Believes that patterns of consistency exist between how musicians function and communicate with each other and the way they perform together and interact musically. Using a recorded example (from early 20th century Egypt) of urban secular music played by a *takht* ensemble, author presents a social analysis of the musician's professional world, and in this light, an interpretation of takht instrumentation, forms and modes of performing.

142. Reyes Schramm, Adelaida. "Ethnic Music, the Urban Area, and Ethnomusicology." *Sociologus*, n.f., 29/2 (1979):1–21.

Major thrust of the author's discussion is directed not toward another definition of "ethnic" but at establishing a need for and proposing components of a common base for discussion, description and explanation. Feels that the dynamics generated by the large population movements in urban areas, that is, the processes by which they select, adopt, adapt, and transform their music, will be the most challenging and the most revealing of the ways in which music changes. Includes a valuable References Cited section (pp. 17–21).

143. ———. "Explorations in Urban Ethnomusicology: Hard Lessons from the Spectacularly Ordinary." *Yearbook for Traditional Music* 14, 1982 (1983):1–14.

Addresses two questions: how do we delineate the object of study in an urban milieu? and, related to the first question, what are the concerns about socio-cultural context? These in turn suggest a third question: what insights into the term, urban ethnomusicology, might be gained through an investigation of the above issues?

144. ———. "Music and Tradition: From Native to Adopted Land Through the Refugee Experience." *Yearbook for Traditional Music* 21 (1989):25–35.

Expounds the thesis that music of refugees requires methodological consideration beyond that given the music and music making of other migrants. As of 1987 the number of worldwide refugees was over 14 million. Poses the question: does their music, as part of their cultural life, qualify for ethnomusicological attention? The author places the question in the context of developing ethnomusicological thought and migration studies in general in order to provide a basis for discussion and to demonstrate the legitimacy of the question on empirical grounds. An aspect of the author's own life experience plays an important role.

145. ———. "The Role of Music in the Interaction of Black Americans and Hispanos in New York City's East Harlem." Ph.D. diss., Columbia University, 1975.

Studies one community, New York City's East Harlem, in order to identify problems specific to it as well as problems it shares with other urban communities, and to explore the methodological implications of these problems. Sources are three types of music-making groups: the formally, informally, and contextually structured. Concludes that the problems posed here can be taken as directives for a method and applied worldwide. The beginning of urban ethnomusicology studies.

146. ———. "Tradition in the Guise of Innovation: Music Among a Refugee Population." *Yearbook for Traditional Music* 18 (1986):91–101.

Motivated by the acceleration of population movements in the modern world, and the technologies that intensify cultural interaction, raises questions concerning tradition and departures from it. Author calls attention to contemporary phenomena which lead one into the area that tradition and innovation share, and suggests restatements of the questions that will take new data into account and stimulate a fresh look at issues of tradition and innovation. Data from the Vietnam refugee population in New Jersey are used as a starting point for a theoretical framework; the Vietnamese New Year celebration, the Tet, was the object of field study.

147. Rice, Timothy. "Aspects of Bulgarian Musical Thought." *Yearbook of the International Folk Music Council* 12 (1980):43–66.

Author delineates the folk taxonomies, terms, and behaviors relevant to a study of Bulgarian musical thought, using data on both singers and instrumentalists. Focus is on musical sounds and structures and the way Bulgarian villagers conceptualize them. Based upon author's fieldwork, article is inspired by semantic misunderstandings between him and his informants.

148. ———. "Toward a Remodeling of Ethnomusicology." *Ethnomusicology* 31/3 (Fall 1987):469–88.

Presents a model based on cognitive anthropology. Inspired by Geertz's *The Interpretation of Cultures* (item 368), author found the "formative processes" he had been seeking and felt that these might supply answers to the following questions: how do people make music or, in its more elaborate form, how do people historically construct, socially maintain and individually create and experience music? Earlier echoes of this model can be found in Herndon and McLeod, Blacking, and Feld. Critical comments and replies by Shelemay, A. Seeger (item 160), Koskoff, Harwood, and R. Crawford follow in the same journal issue.

149. ————. "Understanding Three-Part Singing in Bulgaria: The Interplay of Theory and Experience." *Selected Reports in Ethnomusicology* 7 (1988):43–57.

Shows how assumptions of the observer determine his perception of structure. Supports the advice that a researcher should follow his own instincts about the music he is studying.

* ———— and Robert Falck, eds. *Cross-Cultural Perspectives on Music.* SEE Falck, Robert (item 52).

150. Robertson-De Carbo, Carol E. "Music as Therapy: A Bio-Cultural Problem." *Ethnomusicology* 18/1 (Jan. 1974):31–42.

Discusses the symptomatology and physiology of mental disorders. Intends to corroborate the significance of cultural cognition as demonstrated by the role of music in psychotherapy. Points out that the aim of music therapists in Western culture is to bring about changes in behavior through music; likewise the non-Western curing specialist attempts the same through external stimuli, one of which is music. Some questions remain unanswered: how is music stored in the brain? how do the mediating schemata become altered in the psychotic patient? how does the order in music contribute to the ordering of socio-cultural perceptions? Feels it is important that students of human behavior begin to examine the structures that help determine the performance patterns of man.

151. Robertson, Carol E. "Power and Gender in the Musical Experiences of Women." In *Women and Music in Cross-Cultural Perspective*, ed. by Ellen Koskoff, 225–44. New York: Greenwood Press, 1987. Reprint. Urbana: University of Illinois Press, 1989.

Concerns a broad, comparative view of performance as an instrument of power and gender definition. Musical performance lets us understand how people achieve what they want within their own environment, how they act out their assumptions about each other, and how they challenge authority. Author's arguments lead to a concluding framework of questions that may be put to use in the cross-cultural study of women and music-making. The goal is to strenghten a systematic approach to the relationships between gender, social power, and performance.

152. ———. "'Pulling the Ancestors': Performance Practice and Praxis in Mapuche Ordering." *Ethnomusicology* 23/3 (Sept. 1979):395–416.

Concerns questions of performance practice and the cognitive ramifications of musical communication. Questions of why, what and how. Focuses on the vocal genre of *tayil*, particularly through the Mapuche tenets of time, thought, growth and transformation. Metaphor "pulling the ancestors" refers to act of performing tayil, the explicit manifestation of the patrilineally inherited and shared soul.

153. Ronström, Owe. "Making Use of History: the Revival of the Bagpipe in Sweden in the 1980s." *Yearbook for Traditional Music* 21 (1989):95–108.

Describes and analyzes the process whereby a type of bagpipe was revived and parts of a common historical and cultural heritage were transformed and used in contemporary society for different purposes. The bagpipe was placed in the midst of a set of contrastive processes important at several different levels. These processes are constantly recreating and reshaping the borderlines along which the categorization of "we" and "other" is taking place, in almost totally unpredictable ways.

154. Roseman, Marina. "The Social Structuring of Sound: The Temiar of Peninsular Malaysia." *Ethnomusicology* 28/3 (Sept. 1984):411–45.

Part of a Symposium on Comparative Sociomusicology; follows Feld's article on "Sound Structure . . . " (item 59) with responses from Keil, Robertson, A. Seeger, the Beckers, Gourlay, W. Powers, Ellen Basso and Robert Knox Dentan. Seeks to present the Temiar data on social relations and sonic presentations in a framework that will facilitate future comparisons within various societal, environmental, geographical and historical contexts. In this way, the author feels we can begin to comprehend the significance of sound as it is conceptually informed and socially performed.

155. Rouget, Gilbert. *Music and Trance; a Theory of the Relations between Music and Possession.* Chicago: University of Chicago Press, 1985. Translated from the French, revised by Brunhilde Biebuyck in collaboration with the author.

Examines the association with ritual trance and altered states of consciousness to music. Discusses the nature of the association, whether it is universal or culturally specific, neurophysiologically or symbolically based, and finds no simple answers. Principal types of trance are identified (a typology is developed) but possession trance appears to have the most paradoxical relation to music. Here he believes that music is not so important except in its role to socialize the trance and therefore enable it to attain its full development. Concludes that no simple universal law can explain the relationship; instead their interaction depends on the systems of meaning in each home culture. Concentration upon the cultures of West and Central Africa, but also Latin America, Russia, the Middle East, and Europe. This book has been the subject of two symposiums: one at U.C.L.A. organized by James Porter ("Trance, Music, and Music/Trance Relations: A Symposium," *Pacific Review of Ethnomusicology* 4 [1987]:1–38), and another in Amsterdam organized by the Nederlandse Vereniging voor Etnomusicologie 'Arnold Bake', June 9, 1989.

156. Sakata, Lorraine. "The Concept of Musician in Three Persian-Speaking Areas of Afghanistan." *Asian Music* 8/1 (1976):1–28.

Comparison reveals that the presence and number of hereditary, professional musicians is the largest factor in determining the number and types of terms used in each area. Offers insight into the relationship of various conditions that influence the final conceptualizations of musicians. The more urban the setting, the more strictly the inhabitants view music and musicians, and express their view through formalized concepts, censure and segregation.

157. ————. *Music in the Mind: The Concepts of Music and Musician in Afghanistan.* Kent, Ohio: Kent State University Press, 1983. Two accompanying cassette tapes.

Deals with three different Persian-speaking geographic areas and finds some unified features; shows poetry to be most important of all the arts. Study displays a close relationship between folk and classical musics, and between rural and urban musical genres. Using a cognitive anthropological approach, focuses on informants' musical concepts. Also demonstrates the importance of socio-linguistic variables such as the speaker's language community, status, sex, occupation, and level of sophistication for the semantic analysis of musical terminology.

158. Sanger, Annette. "Music and Musicians, Dance and Dancers: Socio-Musical Interrelationships in Balinese Performance." *Yearbook for Traditional Music* 21 (1989):57–69.

Author examines the interrelationships between Balinese musicians and dancers from a predominantly anthropological perspective. Demonstrates that close links exist at both a conceptual level (in indigenous definitions) and at a practical level in the processes of performance and composition. Using field data from two southern villages, suggests that the relationship between music and dance (musicians and dancers) is unequal; dance and dancers are accorded a higher status. Compares the Balinese with other dance-music contexts in order to test findings.

Schramm, Adelaida. SEE Reyes Schramm, Adelaida

159. Schuyler, Philip D. "Hearts and Minds: Three Attitudes Toward Performance Practice and Music Theory in the Yemen Arab Republic." *Ethnomusicology* 34/1 (Winter 1990):1–18.

Looks at theory from the perspective of three groups of Yemeni musicians who embody the musical elite. Linked to traditional art musics of the Middle East in melodies, meters and forms, Yemeni music developed in relative isolation until the 1960s. Yet a separate system of musical analysis was never created and theory has little influence on musician's discourse. In fact, some musicians feel that there is no place for theory in their music.

The Yemenis' ideas about music, which often take the form of a consistent, coherent system, are far from what they consider to be a science of music.

160. Seeger, Anthony. "Do We Need to Remodel Ethnomusicology?" *Ethnomusicology* 31/3 (Fall 1987):491–95.

Commends Rice's paper read at 1986 S.E.M. Annual Meeting (item 148) for documenting some of the difficulties ethnomusicologists have had applying anthropological approaches to musical performance. Basically agreeing with Rice, the author discusses only three issues: "Merriam's model," developments in anthropology since 1964, and observations on the necessity of constructing a single model for the field of ethnomusicology.

161. ———. "The Role of Sound Archives in Ethnomusicology Today." *Ethnomusicology* 30/2 (Spring/Summer 1986):261–76.

Discusses the perceived, actual, and potential roles of sound archives. Following a general discussion the author makes some concrete suggestions for the future as regards archives, informants, and ethnomusicology as a whole.

162. ———. "'Sing for Your Sister': The Structure and Performance of Suyá *Akia.*" In *The Ethnography of Musical Performance*, ed. by Marcia Herndon and Norma McLeod, 7–42. Norwood: Norwood Editions, 1980.

Suggests one way of answering the questions, "what are they doing" and "why are they doing it *in that particular way,*" is to hypothesize that there are principles common to a society, and the performance of a single genre in its various contexts. Points to the relationship of the *akia* song genre to the dualism in many other spheres of Suyá society.

163. ———. "What Can We Learn When They Sing? Vocal Genres of the Suyá Indians of Central Brazil." *Ethnomusicology* 23/3 (September 1979):373–94.

Relates the singing style of the *akia* genre to the singer's intention to be heard as an individual by certain female relatives, its structure to the overall dualism permeating Suyá life, and other features to specific aspects of the performance context. The *ngere* genre, on the other hand, is a way of expressing the existence and unity of name-based ceremonial groups. Suggests that an important communicative feature of music is its ability to traverse social, psychological, and spatial distances, and that the linguistic emphasis of our own society may not be universal.

164. ———. *Why Suyá Sing: A Musical Anthropology of an Amazonian People*. Cambridge Studies in Ethnomusicology. Cambridge: Cambridge University Press, 1987. Accompanying cassette.

Considers the reasons for the importance of music for the Suyá through an examination of myth telling, speech making, and singing, mainly through one ceremony, the Mouse ceremony. Analyzing the different verbal arts and then focusing on some details of musical performance, he reveals how Suyá singing creates euphoria out of silence, a village community out of a collection of houses, a socialized adult out of a boy, and contributes to the formation of ideas about space, time, and social identity. Perspective is that of musical anthropology (a study of society from the perspective of musical performance) as distinct from an anthropology of music (the application of anthropological methods and concerns to music). Includes a proposed methodology for ethnomusicological study. Feld reviews it as a study that speaks to a broad interdisciplinary audience (*YTM* 21:138).

165. Seeger, Charles. "Music as Concept and as Percept." In *Studies in Musicology 1935–1975*, 31–44. Berkeley: University of California Press, 1977. [Originally published (but later revised) as "Reflections upon a Given Theme: Music in Universal Perspective." *Ethnomusicology* 15/3 (Sept. 1971):385–98].

A chart is presented (here changes exist between the two published papers) that outlines all possible taxonomies and hierarchies expressed in the parameter of speech semantic variance. Argues that musicology should be a speech discipline, and that speech and music are ineluctably related; also that the study of musics other than one's own makes it less likely to distort one's understanding of one's own music.

166. ———. "On the Moods of a Music Logic." *Journal of the American Musicological Society* 13 (1960):224–61. Reprinted in *Studies in Musicology*: 64–101.

Concerns rationalizing music, and to that end seeks some sort of order. Proposes that the units of music design and music logic can be regarded as identical, and that they can be presented in a speech rationale as a single, partly closed system, equally of patterns of design and moods of logic.

167. ———. "On the Tasks of Musicology." *Ethnomusicology* 7/3 (Sept. 1963):214–15.

Comments on Merriam's "Purposes of Ethnomusicology" (item 108). Very critical of what he thinks are Merriam's too narrow views. Proposes his own ideas concerning the two major reasons for ethnomusicological study.

* ———. "Reflections upon a Given Theme" SEE "Music as Concept and as Percept" (item 165).

168. ———. "Reflections Upon a Given Topic: Music in Universal Perspective." *Ethnomusicology* 15/3 (Sept. 1971):385–98.

Part of the S.E.M. Panel on Universals, 1970 (see also List, item 92; Wachsmann, item 194; and McAllester, item 97). Presents the author's outline of a taxonomy-hierarchy of the parameter of speech semantic variance, which he calls an abstract-universal-concept and concrete-particular-percept. An improved version of the original chart is presented with organized comment.

169. ———. "Semantic, Logical and Political Considerations Bearing upon Research into Ethnomusicology." *Ethnomusicology* 5/2 (May 1961):77–80.

Dissects the term ethnomusicology, its logic, and its politics with appropriate recommendations. Lays the groundwork for dropping the "ethno" part of the word for the study of all musics. Some consider his view of music in three general contextual classes ("concept" in speech communication, "phenomenon" in nature, and "communicatory medium" in itself like speech) as a theoretical research model (item 110).

170. ———. *Studies in Musicology, 1935–1975*. Berkeley: University of California Press, 1977.

The republication of eighteen essays on systematic and historical musicology, and a mixture of the two. The author's introduction, "Systematic (Synchronic) and Historical (Diachronic) Orientations in Musicology" goes far to help explain the complexities of his philosophy and writing. In one case, "Music as Concept and as Precept" (item 165), Seeger revised and retitled an earlier work.

171. ———. "Toward a Unitary Field Theory for Musicology." *Selected Reports* (Los Angeles: UCLA Institute of Ethnomusicology) 1/3 (1970):171–210. [Reprinted in *Studies in Musicology* 1977:102–38.]

Imaginary interrogation of the author by Boris Kremenliev and a student involving the construction of a unitary field theory made up of five universes: speech, music, individuality, culture, and physics.

172. ———. "Tractatus Esthetico-Semioticus." *Current Thought in Musicology*, edited by J.W. Grubbs, 1–39. Austin and London: University of Texas Press, 1976. Symposia in the Arts and the Humanities, no. 4. o.p.

The result of a symposium held at the University of Texas in 1971. Presents a general theory in accord with which the communicatory systems of man (the arts and crafts), and their cultivation in a common physical and cultural context may be presented with the least distortion by the art of speech. The main framework—the distinction of three modes of communication, discursive, logical, and mystical—offers musicologists a valuable approach to the evaluation of composers' achievements. The carrying out of these ideas suggests many new channels for musicological thought. Compare with Boilès' "Universals of Musical Behavior" (item 46).

173. Shelemay, Kay Kaufman. *Music, Ritual, and Falasha History.* Ethiopian series monograph no. 17. East Lansing: Michigan State University, African Studies Center, 1986.

Contributes to ethnomusicology in general as well as to Jewish culture in particular, although several reviewers were critical. Uses a strict *emic* approach to help unravel detailed liturgical sections. This approach could be applied to other cultures in order to show links between their present situation and their historical roots through traditional music.

174. Silver, Brian. "On Becoming an Ustad: Six Life Sketches in the Evolution of a Gharana." *Asian Music* 7/2 (1976):27–58. With Appendix "The Historical Background of Indore and Satellite Courts" by R. Arnold Burghardt, pp. 51–3.

Embodies two concerns: 1) to explore the different musical and social factors which may combine in varying formulae to constitute *ustadi* — the state of being an ustad; and 2) to explore the means by which a collective incidence of ustadi may develop into the social tradition of the gharana.

175. Slobin, Mark. *Chosen Voices: the Story of the American Cantorate.* Urbana: University of Illinois Press, 1989. An accompanying cassette tape.

Title is one of the keys to the ethnomusicological approach with which the author unifies his study. On one level are the *hazzanim* (cantors) chosen by the community through a complex process. Interviews with hundreds of cantors in the mid-1980s provides the data. The cantorate watches over their tradition and stewards the careers of member cantors in a uniquely American way. Examines the dualities that lead to this distinctive characteristic. Challenges are sprinkled throughout, e.g., to compare cantorial music with other traditions, and to decry the lack of sufficient research in other traditions to make such a comparison possible. Ultimate challenge may be for the cantorate itself, whose response could be the point of departure for another study (the members bought out the first print-run within weeks after the book's appearance). Reviewed by Bohlman (*EM* 34/2:303–6).

176. ———. "The Evolution of a Musical Symbol in Yiddish Culture." In *Studies in Jewish Folklore*, ed. by Frank Talmage, 313–42. Cambridge, Mass.: Association for Jewish Studies, 1980.

Proceedings of a Regional Conference of the Association for Jewish Studies held at Spertus College of Judaica, Chicago, May 1977. Concerns the evolution of a particular musical symbol—two melody-types with augmented 2nd/raised 4th intervals termed *frigish* (by Jewish musicians) and "Ukrainian Doric" (by Idelsohn)—in Eastern European Jewish culture. Deals with their initial use in an Old World folk music context, on through Yiddish popular music in the late 19th century, up to the New World in the early 20th century. Concludes with remarks on the recent biography of the symbol since the 1920s. Key moments in the life-cycle of the musical symbol are examined.

177. ———. *Music in the Culture of Northern Afghanistan.* Viking Fund Publications in Anthropology, 54. Tucson: University of Arizona Press, 1976.

Based on his dissertation on instrumental music, the author focuses on a single cultural trait—music—as it illuminates the patterns of interethnic contact in Northern Afghanistan. Presents two kinds of data: 1) descriptive information about the music, including a comprehensive listing of musical instruments and an analytical presentation of genres and styles, and 2) an examination both of the musical traits (attitudes, repertoires, instruments) that are shared by two or more ethnic groups, and of those discrete elements that occur in the music of only one ethnic group and thus mark off music subcultures.

178. ———. *Tenement Songs; the Popular Music of the Jewish Immigrants.* Music in American Life Series. Urbana: University of Illinois Press, 1982. Accompanying cassette recording.

Traces the songs which flourished during the Jewish migration to the U.S. (1880–1920) in an effort to keep them in the memory of American Jewry. Focusing on the sheet-music industry, the author shows how closely linked this music was to the Yiddish theater. Includes a discussion of musical style and song texts.

179. Stockmann, Erich. "The Diffusion of Musical Instruments as an Interethnic Process of Communication." *Yearbook of the International Folk Music Council* 3, 1971 (1972):128–37.

Attempts to apply the methods of cybernetics, information theory and semiotics to the solution of research problems in organology. Includes knowledge about the making, handling and function of musical instruments between two ethnic groups. Offers several methodological conclusions concerning interethnic relations.

180. Stone, Ruth M. *Dried Millet Breaking: Time, Words, and Story in the Woi Epic of the Kpelle.* Bloomington: Indiana University Press, 1988.

The author's second book (cf. item 181) on the performance genres of the Kpelle people. It is a result of her observation fifteen years ago that, as she followed a theme, it would suddenly shift to another topic. Discusses Kpelle ideas of time as found in the *woi-meni-pele*, an epic about the hero Woi, a mythic "everyman" that combines singing, narration, dramatic performance and instrumental accompaniment. Time concepts include: rhythms of music sound, placement of music text, the larger event flow, and the movement of time for both the individual and the family. Book is organized according to themes/patterns that the Kpelle themselves consider important for the consideration of timing principles. Work is premised on the "emic" paradigm and addresses the dynamic process/product of the performance artifact in terms of its cultural context. Tries to fuse the sound-oriented and behavior-oriented approaches to ethnomusicology. Concludes that a new praxis for ethnomusicology has been demonstrated as well as a new model by which to understand African music. Locke's review (*EM* 34:172–4) felt that these goals were not sufficiently demonstrated.

181. ———. *Let the Inside Be Sweet: The Interpretation of Music Event among the Kpelle of Liberia.* Bloomington: Indiana University Press, 1982.

Uses the music event among the Kpelle people as the focal study object as well as the technique of feedback interviews.

Maintains that social relations and interactions normally constrained are permitted and encouraged in musical interaction. A methodical endeavor to bring together the study sounds of performance ("sound" ethnomusicology) and the behavior of performers and audiences ("behavior" ethnomusicology). Author's study background in both anthropology and folklore are combined in an exploration of the "music event," first as a theoretical construct and then in a particular field study application. Concludes that music events are dynamically created by selecting and manipulating facets of everyday life. Music both reflects and restructures culture, and can only be understood as we learn to interpret nuance, subtlety, and ambiguity in the processual creation of music performances. Theoretical conclusions draw from symbolic interactionism and semiotic-cybernetic communication. Reviewed by DjeDje in *EM* 27/3:544–6.

182. Sugarman, Jane C. "Making *Muabet*: The Social Basis of Singing among Prespa Albanian Men." *Selected Reports in Ethnomusicology* 7 (1988):1–42.

Analyzes men's gatherings in an emigré community living in North America using the conceptualization of music as a basic framework. Shows how concepts of honor (*nder*), order (*radhe*), and intimacy (*muabet*) are used to structure singing events and how singing serves to reaffirm the central position of such concepts within the community's meaning system.

183. ———. "The Nightingale and the Partridge: Singing and Gender among Prespa Albanians." *Ethnomusicology* 33/2 (Spring/Summer 1989):191–215.

Combines ideas from performance theory with music and gender studies. Gender aspects and musical practice are seen to exist in a dialectical relationship to each other, each functioning as a mutually determining aspect of the Prespa social whole. Winner of the 1987 Seeger Prize.

184. Titon, Jeff Todd, ed. *Worlds of Music; an Introduction to the Music of the World's Peoples*. New York: Schirmer, 1984. Two accompanying cassette tapes.

An introductory textbook based on the collaborative efforts of Titon, James Koetting, David McAllester, David B. Reck, and Mark Slobin. Instead of a world survey it concentrates on a small number of case studies according to six guiding principles. Although intended as a basic text for courses in the analysis of music cultures, the book offers much more. Reviewed by Shumway (*EM* 30/2:355). A second edition including extensively revised and expanded chapters and new case studies of the musics of Indonesia, Oceania, and Asia is forthcoming.

185. Tolbert, Elizabeth. "On Beyond Zebra: Some Theoretical Considerations of Emotion and Meaning in Music." *Pacific Review of Ethnomusicology* 4 (1987):75–97.

Explores the hypothetical entities in research that exist after the limits of the everyday alphabet have been exhausted. Considers the iconic nature of music in greater detail, especially iconicity with biological and cosmological systems. Attempts to show that meaning in music is not found in form alone, nor as an appendage to a certain cultural context, but rather in the intersection of psychobiological and cultural experience. This in turn emerges from the exigencies of sacred ritual and its concurrent unusual modes of perception. Draws from her study of the Finnish *Karelian* lament to illustrate layers of meaning in a musical context.

186. ———. "Women Cry with Words: Symbolization of Affect in the Karelian Lament." *Yearbook for Traditional Music* 22 (1990):80–105.

Based upon research with Karelian women (eastern Finland and Soviet Karelia) now living in Finland, about an almost forgotten lament genre, *itkuvirsi*. Addresses the expressive means in which "crying with words" becomes the ritualized crying of the lament. Concerns in particular how emotion is communicated in performance, especially how the lament becomes a "sign vehicle" for effect. Explores both textual and musical components, and proposes a model of three different musical levels of form (from macro to micro, the lament phrase, lament prosody, and the symbolic system). Several influences acknowledged, e.g., Caraveli-Chaves, Feld, Radcliffe-Brown, as well as Finnish and

Soviet scholars. See Vaughn (item 315) who used Tolbert's field data as the basis for her time series analysis applied to digitized melody.

187. Turino, Thomas. "The Coherence of Social Style and Musical Creation Among the Aymara in Southern Peru." *Ethnomusicology* 33/1 (1989)1–30.

Using an ethnographic approach, examines musical practices, aesthetics, and creation among the Aymara in Peru, as one realm in which their notions of the "natural" are clearly articulated. Discusses instruments and performance techniques, the social and musical organization of ensembles, the compositional process, and the form of the music itself in order to illustrate the homologous relationship between musical culture and behavior, forms and values in other realms of activity.

188. ———. "The Music of Andean Migrants in Lima, Peru: Demographics, Social Power, and Style." *Latin American Music Review* 9/2 (1988):127–50.

From research conducted among migrants in Lima and indigenous Andeans at home in Puno, Peru between November 1984 and July 1986. Focuses on the history of Andean music in the Peruvian capital. Contrary to expectations (because of assimilation, urbanization and Westernization due to the acceleration of Andean migrants into Lima), a growing presence of regionally specific, traditional highland music evidences itself, as well as an increase in migrant control over their own cultural resources. Demographic shift is a partial explanation; more important is an alteration in the power relations between the dominant criollo group and the Andean migrants.

189. ———. "Structure, Context and Strategy in Musical Ethnography." *Ethnomusicology* 34/3 (Fall 1990):399–412.

Part of a symposium on the Representation of Musical Practice and the Practice of Representation, S.E.M. Annual Meeting, 1989 (see also Blum, item 41; Waterman, item 195; and Grenier and Guilbault, item 63). Considers "practice theory" (a response to the current crisis of ethnographic representation in regard to its value as well as its more problematic aspects for musical ethnographers). Takes the work of Bourdieu and De Certeau as points of departure. Illustrated by author's field experience among Aymara in southern Peru, 1986, especially the Fiesta de la Cruz. In a particularly significant section, "The Practice of Ethnomusicological Representation," author points to several factors that have influenced informants' representation of their musical culture to the fieldworker and have found their way thence into the descriptive and analytical literature.

190. Vander, Judith. *Ghost Dance Songs and Religion of a Wind River Shoshone Woman*. Monograph Series in Ethnomusicology, no. 4. Los Angeles: Program in Ethnomusicology, U.C.L.A. Department of Music, 1986.

Focuses on seventeen songs of one elderly woman, Emily Hill, whose knowledge of the repertoire is comparatively large. Chapters on the *naraya* (Shoshone Ghost Dance), musical analysis, textual analysis, and the *naraya* today. The beliefs that shaped the ceremony in the past, even though it is no longer performed, still influence religious ceremonies and those living today.

191. ———. *Songprints; the Musical Experience of Five Shoshone Women*. Urbana: University of Illinois Press, 1988. Accompanying cassette tape.

Book's title derives from the term for each singer's song repertoire distinctive to her culture, age, and personality. The women represent different generations. Placed in context of social and religous ceremonies to offer insights into rise of the Native American Church, the emergence and popularity of the contemporary *powwow* and the changing, enlarged role of women. Analyzes 75 songs. Provides new material on Ghost Dance songs and performances, mainly through discussions with the two older women who saw it performed.

192. Wachsmann, Klaus P. "Criteria for Acculturation." *Report of the Eighth Congress of the International Musicological Society, New York, 1961*, vol. 1, Papers, 139–49. Kassel: Bärenreiter, 1961.

Studies the implications of the term acculturation for music and musicology, restricting references to the Ganda tribe of East Africa. Describes the interest in dynamic processes that both musicologists and anthropologists have in common. Discussion of the problems affecting the study of "long-term cultural development" in music. Suggests that general trends may make themselves felt in the process of acculturation. Promotes discussion on the means and distinguishing marks, i.e., criteria, by which acculturation in music can be characterized.

193. ———, ed. *Essays on Music and History in Africa*. Evanston: Northwestern University Press, 1971.

The papers are grouped geographically except for the "Music and History" section. Writers apply themselves to the common understanding that they would search for musical evidence side by side with archaeological, historical and similar material, correlate these wherever possible, and in general, explore how music and history can mutually define and illuminate each other. From papers read at the Symposium on Music and History in Africa and Asia in 1962, plus two essays from the African Studies Association meeting in Montreal, 1969.

194. ———. "Universal Perspectives in Music." *Ethnomusicology* 15/3 (Sept. 1971):381–4.

From the 1970 S.E.M. Panel on Universals (see also List, item 92; McAllester, item 97; and Seeger, item 168). Author considers the philosophical implications of McAllester's points. Concludes that music is a special kind of time and the creation of musical time a universal occupation of man.

195. Waterman, Christopher A. "'Our Tradition is a Very Modern Tradition': Popular Music and the Construction of Pan-Yoruba Identity." *Ethnomusicology* 34/3 (Fall 1990):367–79.

Part of a symposium on the Representation of Musical Practice and the Practice of Representation, S.E.M., 1989 (see also Blum, item 41; Grenier and Guilbault, item 63; and Turino, item 189). Deals with the role of contemporary popular music in the production of cultural identity among the Yoruba of southwestern

Nigeria. Argument rests on the axiom that all human identities, no matter how deeply felt, are from an historical point of view mixed, relational, and conjunctural (see Clifford, item 347). Suggests drawing an analytical distinction between *invented traditions* and everyday processes of *stereotypic reproduction*. Cautions that the past can never be a limitless and plastic resource, neither etched in stone nor spun out of thin air ("Our Yoruba tradition is a very modern tradition").

196. Zemp, Hugo. "'Are'are Classification of Musical Types and Instruments." *Ethnomusicology* 22/1 (Jan. 1978):37–67.

Aim of this approach deriving from cognitive anthropology is to examine a folk classification which, besides having interest in itself, may give new insights into different aspects of musical thinking. Concludes that the study of folk classification is a first step to understanding what constitutes music for a society, after which one no longer poses the question concerning the nature of music in the same terms. The first of two articles (see item 197).

197. ———. "Aspects of 'Are'are Musical Theory." *Ethnomusicology* 23/1 (Jan. 1979):5–48.

Continuation of earlier article (item 196). Analysis is limited to the music of panpipe ensembles. Studies in detail the concept of interval in classifying musical instruments and musical segmentation and the concept of polyphonic organization.

198. ———. *Musique Dan: La Musique dans la pensée et la vie sociale d'une société africaine.* Cahiers de l'homme Ethnologie-Geographie-Linguistique, 11. Paris: Mouton, 1971.

A penetrating descriptive analysis of the musical material culture, concepts and behaviors of an African people. Merriam described it as one of the best books on African music, if not the best of its particular genre (*EM* 17:139–41).

III. FIELDWORK METHOD
AND TECHNIQUE

199. Baily, John. "ICTM Colloquium on Film and Video." *Yearbook for Traditional Music* 20/1 (1988):193–98.

Brings together ethnomusicologists committed to using film and video for scholarly purposes in order to discuss current issues. The two uses of film, for scientific purposes and for communication to both specialists and the general audience, revealed three inter-related factors common to both types: the conception and intention of the filmmaker, the methods of shooting and editing the film, and the destination of the footage. Contributors include Gerhard Kubik and Hugo Zemp, who both use film but in different ways.

200. Baron, Robert. "Syncretism and Ideology: Latin New York Salsa Musicians." *Western Folklore* 36/3 (May 1977):209–25.

Based on the observation that Salsa musicians draw upon and rework tradition while experimenting with the music of several different Latin ethnic groups in New York City. Considers changes in instrumentation, use of musical and linguistic code-switching, and of musical forms associated with popular cultures as behavioral realizations of ideologies bound up with syncretic processes. Traditions assume new meanings. Salsa musicians seek to maintain continuity with forms from the past while adapting new ones marked by rapid culture contact and commercial pressures.

201. Barth, Fredrik, ed. *Ethnic Groups and Boundaries: the Social Organization of Culture Difference.* rev. Little, Brown Series in Anthropology. Boston: Little, Brown, 1969; Oslo: Universitetsforlaget, 1982.

Essays from a symposium in which Scandinavian social anthropologists cooperated in a joint effort to further the analysis of ethnic groups. Barth's introduction presents his original ideas and the ensuing results of the discussion. Essays concern the problems of ethnic groups and their persistence. Two discoveries regarding the character of ethnic boundaries emerge: 1) boundaries persist despite a flow of people across them, and 2) stable, persisting and often vitally important social relations are maintained across these boundaries and are frequently based on dichotomized ethnic statuses.

202. Becker, Howard. "Photography and Sociology." *Studies in the Anthropology of Visual Communication* 1/1 (1974):3–26.

A sociological guide for those social scientists and photographers who are dissatisfied with their current procedures and want to try something new. Shows sociologists with no interest in photographic work that they can learn something, particularly how to really look at a photograph. Describes photographer's techniques for making different photographic statements and for using varying quantities of images to make these statements. Especially useful is the discussion (pp. 12–14) demonstrating ways in which sociological ideas and theory can be brought together with photographic explorations of society. Concludes with a sizeable list of useful literature.

203. Bellman, Beryl Larrt and Bennetta Jules-Rosette. *A Paradigm for Looking: Cross-Cultural Research with Visual Media.* Norwood, N.J.: Ablex Pub. Corp., 1977.

Studies the introduction of media to two African communities. Authors often asked informants to videotape or film different kinds of social interactions, palavers, and rituals. Discovered not only that the films contributed important information to the analysis, but that they actually influenced the direction taken in analysis. Two sections, "Some methodologies for understanding media" (pp. 17–25) and "A paradigm for looking, film and video in two communities" (pp. 190–205), are especially useful.

* SEE ALSO Berliner, Paul. *The Soul of Mbira* (item 30).

204. Blacking, John. "Field Work in African Music." In *Reflections on Afro-American Music*, edited by Dominique-René deLerma, 207–21. Kent: Kent State University Press, 1973.

Written in a personal style at the time when the author was first teaching in the U.S. Stresses techniques and experiences in relation to three different theoretical objectives: 1) the collection of musical samples (he rejects analysis derived from musical sound alone), 2) the intensive study of a musical tradition with special reference to the function of music as an aspect of the behavior of man in society, and 3) the intensive study of a musical tradition as a system of musical cognitive and social processes which in turn are part of, or are related to, the social and cultural system of the music maker.

205. Carpenter, Inta Gale, ed. "Folklorists in the City: The Urban Field Experience." *Folklore Forum* 11/3 (1978):195–320.

Articles resulting from team research (from the Folklore Institute, Bloomington, Indiana University) in the Calumet Region of northwest Indiana (nicknamed "the Gary Gang") in the summer of 1975. Carpenter's introduction (pp. 195–7) mentions a few of the topics and questions raised by this urban field experience. Recommended articles are: Richard M. Dorson's "Team Fieldwork" (pp. 220–33), Thomas Adler's "When Fieldwork Becomes Fieldshock" (pp. 234–44), Adrienne Lanier Seward's "Some Dilemmas of Fieldwork: a Personal Statement" (pp. 245–53), Richard March's "How I Became 'The TV Man': Video Fieldwork in the Calumet Region" (pp. 254–64), Elena Bradunas' "From the Familiar to the Unknown: a Fieldwork's Progression" (pp. 273–89), and John Hasse's "Field Specifics Learned First-Hand in the City" (pp. 290–314).

206. Collier, John Jr. and Malcolm Collier. *Visual Anthropology: Photography as a Research Method*. New York: Holt, Rinehart and Winston, 1967. Rev. and expanded. Albuquerque: University of New Mexico Press, 1986.

In his foreword, Edward T. Hall makes the point that the visual anthropologist needs to identify the structure points in the system which he is studying as well as its contextual components.

This is a manual on the two interlocked processes of observation: first how to get information on film, and second, how to release it.

207. Crick, Malcolm. "Anthropological Field Research, Meaning Creation and Knowledge Construction." In *Semantic Anthropology,* edited by David Parkin, 15–37. A.S.A. Monograph 22. London: Academic Press, 1982.

Concerns what anthropologists have to say about their own professional practices, particularly fieldwork and the creative activities that occur during and after it. Largely looks at several aspects of the anthropological self in the ethnographic context: being an outsider, the rules of fieldwork, and observations on the context of the situation. Stresses importance of the anthropologist creating an identity for himself in the field and shows concern for the transition period between fieldwork and writing. Notes other influences on the intellectual atmosphere: institutional (university), research monies and grants, influence of senior academicians on juniors, and the "feudal" structure of academe.

208. Dauer, Alphons M. "Research Films in Ethnomusicology: Aims and Achievements." *Yearbook of the International Folk Music Council* 1, 1969 (1971):226–33.

Brief description of the Göttingen Institut für den Wissenschaftlichen Film project, which in 1963 began making documentary films of various ethnic groups. Expeditions to Thailand, Chad, Hadramout and the Ivory Coast resulted in more than 200 films. Information about equipment and method is included, as well as examples of Kubik's photogrammetry on a grid graph for the transcription of Mangivilo xylophone music (Northern Mozambique), and Dauer's Western staff notation of dance music from Southeastern Sahara, achieved through motion-analysis by slow projection and enumeration of stills.

209. Davis, Cullom, Kathryn Back and Kay MacLean. *Oral History: From Tape to Type.* Chicago: American Library Association, 1977.

Includes chapters on the collecting process (preparations and interviewing). Conceived as a guide for small or beginning oral history programs. Includes sample interview sheets and other data sheets. Places some emphasis on the use of the tape recorder.

210. Dumont, Jean-Paul. *The Headman and I: Ambiguity and Ambivalence in the Fieldworking Experience.* Texas Pan American series. Austin: University of Texas Press, 1978.

Based on fieldwork with the Panare Indians of Venezuelan Guiana (see especially pp. 3–13). Writing in an easy, frank style, author employs insider/outsider interaction approach. Wishes to continue to observe his informants but is also interested in how they observe him.

211. Feld, Steven. "Avant Propos: Jean Rouch." *Studies in the Anthropology of Visual Communication* 1/1 (1974):35–6.

Author, himself an ethnomusicologist and anthropologist-filmmaker, translated four articles of Jean Rouch, the French ethnographer and filmmaker. This is an introduction to the translations, which were scheduled to appear in the first four issues of *Studies in the Anthropology of Visual Communication.* Pinpoints the considerable contributions of Rouch and considers his dual competence as ethnographer and filmmaker to be unusual.

212. ———. "Ethnomusicology and Visual Communication." *Ethnomusicology* 20/2 (May 1976):293–325.

Summarizes the development of ethnomusicological interest in film (in the U.S., France and Germany), how it is used (through discussions in reviews), a critique of the "pretty picture" tradition, and moving onwards to the more current "anthropology of visual communication" theory and method. Also remarks on film as an aid to transcription. Includes a substantial bibliography (pp. 317–23). Criticizes the fact that there is innovative and exciting potential for film in ethnomusicological work, but that realizing this potential requires a kind of conceptual clarity not currently prevalent.

* SEE ALSO ———. *Sound and Sentiment* (item 57).

213. Fischer, Eberhard and Noa Zanolli. "Das Problem der Kulturdarstellung: Vorschläge zur Methode der Ethnographie." *Sociologus* n.f. 18/1 (1968):1–20.

Concerns the ordering of information in cultural description. Stresses the need for a theoretical foundation in ethnographic method, based on various categorical distinctions. Of these the most fundamental are notative order (nonevaluative observations from outside a culture) and intentional order (statements from within a culture). Advises that the analysis of material gathered and classified in this way should then be conducted as objectively as possible, preferably by means of a standardized coding system for electronic computers.

214. Foster, George M. and Robert V. Kemper. *Anthropologists in Cities*. Boston: Little, Brown, 1974.

Contains ten essays, by different authors, growing out of a graduate seminar on urbanization at U.C. Berkeley. Study was planned to explore the patterns and regularities that anthropologists have noted in the urbanization process in various parts of the world. Aims at answering students' questions about conducting urban fieldwork.

* SEE ALSO Geertz, Clifford. *The Interpretation of Cultures* (item 368).

215. Georges, Robert A. and Michael Owen Jones. *People Studying People: The Human Element in Fieldwork*. Berkeley: University of California Press, 1980.

Traces the thread of personal relations between researchers and their subjects out of which the fabric of fieldwork is woven. Makes the point that individuals conducting research can be human (not only detached and objective).

216. Gibbs, Jack P. *Sociological Theory Construction*. Hinsdale, Ill.: The Dryden Press, 1972.

Proposes a mode of formal theory construction, not a survey of sociological theories. Believes such construction is essential for the progress of sociology, but feels basic issues have been ignored. Three arguments underlie the proposed scheme: 1) theories should be stated formally, 2) they should be testable, and 3) predictive power should be the primary criterion for accessing theories.

217. Goldstein, Kenneth S. *A Guide for Field Workers in Folklore.* Hatboro, N.J.: Folklore Associates; London: Jenkins, 1964.

A self-trained folklorist discusses collecting methods that would satisfactorily supply answers to certain field problems. After finding little available literature in folklore and anthropology, the author establishes his own methodology, borrowing heavily from ethnology. Chapters deal with problem statement and analysis, time consideration, pre-field preparations, rapport establishment maintenance, observation collecting methods, interview collecting methods, supplementary field methods, and the motivation and remuneration of informants.

218. Gombrich, E. H. *The Image and the Eye; Further Studies in the Psychology of Pictorial Representation.* Oxford: Phaidon, 1982.

Builds on his papers in *Art and Illusion,* which called attention to visual tools such as photography, diagrams and maps. Notes in particular an increasing interest in the study of perception.

219. Gorden, Raymond L. *Interviewing: Strategy, Techniques, and Tactics.* The Dorsey series in Sociology. 3rd ed. Homewood, Ill.: Dorsey Press, 1980.

Presents a spectrum of basic processes involved in obtaining valid and reliable information from an informant through interviews. Central focus is on the information-gathering interview as distinct from the therapeutic or persuasive interview. The latter types are dealt with as applicable to collecting certain types of information. Book is based on certain assumptions: a) the reader wants to become a more effective interviewer, b) improvement depends upon combining conceptual understanding and skill development, and c) both the understanding of concepts and the development of skills come with active participation and practice. Includes laboratory problems.

* SEE ALSO Gourlay, Kenneth. "Towards a Reassessment . . . " (item 62).

220. Hall, Edward T. *Beyond Culture*. Garden City, New York: Doubleday, 1976; New York: Anchor Press, 1981.

    In relation to kinesics and synchrony, describes William Condon's frame-by-frame analysis of 16mm films and states that, as a result, music and dance can now be interpreted differently. Links within the specific culture where the movements occur are specific and marked. High-sync, high-context cultures are identified as well as low-sync, low-context cultures. Concludes that the language of behavior is extremely subtle. Particularly recommended is "Rhythm and body movement" (pp. 61–73).

221. Herndon, Marcia and Norma McLeod. *Field Manual for Ethnomusicology*. Norwood, Pa.: Norwood Editions, 1983.

    Conscientious text covering the gamut of fieldwork except for the technical aspect. Points out that the gathering of information in the field is undoubtedly the most important aspect of ethnomusicology today. Stresses minimizing the subjectivity of synchronic field research. Though the book might seem to take itself too seriously, the reader is advised in the final paragraph that the best preparation is to develop common sense, wit, curiosity, flexibility, and a healthy sense of humor.

222. Honoré, Paul M. *A Handbook of Sound Recording: A Text for Motion Picture and General Sound Recording*. South Brunswick N.J.: A.S. Barnes, 1980.

    Although intended to acquaint the professional filmmaker with the fundamentals of putting together a motion picture sound track provides reliable information for anyone who needs basic practice information, such as how to communicate with a recording engineer, and how to spot and correct any trouble. Chapters are sequentially ordered and there is a 7–page index for easy reference.

* SEE ALSO Hood, Mantle. *The Ethnomusicologist* (item 6).

223. Ives, Edward D. *The Tape-Recorded Interview: A Manual for Field Workers in Folklore and Oral History.* Rev. and enl. ed. Knoxville: University of Tennessee Press, 1980.

Keeps two themes in mind: good annotating techniques at every step and dealing with the common man. The research method involves two separate but interrelated activities: 1) going into the field for extended, tape-recorded interviews with people about some aspect of their experience and 2) processing the tape produced so that its contents will be easily available, not only to you but to others who wish to use it in their own research or to check the accuracy of yours. A good beginning text for the novice fieldworker concentrating on taped interview material.

224. Jackson, Bruce. *Fieldwork.* Urbana, Ill.: University of Illinois Press, 1987.

Designed to serve anyone who wants to know what fieldwork is about. Includes how fieldworkers define their function, how they deal with people they meet in the field, and how they capture for later use media records of what transpired in their presence. Much of the book deals with specific and practical matters. Considers awareness of context critical for all fieldworkers in the human sciences. Author trained at Indiana University and the Archive of Traditional Music.

225. Johnson, Allen W. *Quantification in Cultural Anthropology; an Introduction to Research Design.* Stanford: Stanford University Press, 1978.

Concentrates on research designs that have faced the difficulties of translating anthropological theories into operational, usually quantitative, data gathering. Written as a textbook for teaching research methods to anthropologists. Contains examples that may be useful in designing a project. Compare with Lofland's qualitative method (item 238).

226. Johnson, John M. *Doing Field Research.* New York: Free Press [Macmillan], 1975. Also in paper, 1978.

Detailed description and analysis of a sociological field research project. Author investigated social welfare activities in five offices of two large metropolitan departments of public welfare. Book has three main parts: 1) the major arguments in the traditional methodological literature about the problems of conducting field research, 2) the research situation during author's field observations, and 3) comparison of traditional conceptions of field research practice and author's personal experience within the context of current debates on social science objectivity. "Gaining and managing entree in field research" (pp. 50–81) is particularly useful.

227. Junker, Buford Helmholz. *Field Work; an Introduction to the Social Sciences.* Chicago: University of Chicago Press, 1960.

Treats fieldwork as applied sociology in referring to observation of people *in situ.* Author worked in a prison among other places, and has done fieldwork on fieldwork.

228. Kaeppler, Adrienne L. "Method and Theory in Analyzing Dance Structure with an Analysis of Tongan Dance." *Ethnomusicology* 16/2 (1972):173–217.

Describes her method in compiling an inventory of significant movements in a dance tradition. Uses terminology adopted or derived from linguistic analysis, mainly the kinemes, units treated as comparable to phonemes, that is, elements selected from all possible human movements and positions, and are recognized as significant by people of a given dance tradition.

229. Kaplan, Abraham. *The Conduct of Inquiry; Methodology for Behavioral Science.* Chandler Publications in Anthropology and Sociology. San Francisco: Chandler Publishing Co., 1964.

Author, a philosopher, conducts a systematic, rounded, and wide-ranging inquiry into behavioral science. Addresses himself to the methodology of behavioral science in the broad sense of both science and methodology.

   * SEE ALSO Keil, Charles. *Tiv Song* (item 85).

230. Kidder, Louise H. and Charles M. Judd. *Research Methods in Social Relations.* 5th ed. New York: Holt, Rinehart and Winston, 1986.

Introduces a broad range of methodological approaches representative of various social science disciplines. Author is committed to conveying an understanding of research methods. Focuses attention on major issues of interpretation and validity that have broad applicability to many decision-making contexts. Chapter 8 is devoted to "Field Work and Participant Observation: Studying Particular People and Places." Published by the Society for the Psychological Study of Social Issues.

231. Koning, Jos. "The Fieldworker as Performer: Fieldwork Objectives and Social Roles in County Clare, Ireland." *Ethnomusicology* 24/3 (Sept. 1980):417–29.

A re-evaluation of the techniques used in his earlier research, seen in the perspective of their present use. Author describes the usefulness of being a fiddle player himself in attempting to understand a regional style in the west of Ireland.

232. ———. "'That Old Plaintive Touch': On the Relation Between Tonality in Irish Traditional Dance-Music and the Left Hand Technique of Fiddlers in East Co. Clare, Ireland." In *Studia Instrumentorum Musicae Popularis* 6 (1979):80–4. Stockholm: Musikhistoriska museet.

One of the few recent studies on music conceptualization in Western folk traditions. Author discusses concepts of tonality in the left hand technique of fiddling as practiced in Feakle, Co. Clare, Ireland. As a fiddle-player himself, author uses participant observation to solve problems of musical style and technique.

233. Leach, Edmund. *Social Anthropology.* London: Fontana; Oxford University Press, 1982.

Trained in mathematics and engineering, author describes his kind of social anthropology: essentially a demonstration that when an individual progresses through time, from social state A to social state B, the procession is always of the continuous/discontinuous kind. Not so much about structuralism as the different kinds of anthropological influence that converged in his thinking. Chapter 4, "My Kind of Anthropology," is particularly relevant because he feels that real understanding of what anthropologists do comes from doing it oneself.

234. Leeds, Anthony. "The Anthropology of Cities: Some Methodological Issues." In *Urban Anthropology: Research Perspectives and Strategies,* edited by Elizabeth M. Eddy, 31–47. Athens: University of Georgia Press, 1968. No. 2 of the Southern Anthropological Society Proceedings.

Concerns what an anthropologist undertakes in an urban field situation. Critical of previous work, author notes that former research has failed to show mutual effects between groups under study and the city in which they are immersed. Uses his study of *favelas* in Rio de Janeiro to illustrate the logistical constraints of working in only a few sites in a limited amount of time. Advises the ethnographer to keep a single synthetic framework in mind in trying to attain some control over all the relevant entities. The generation of such a synthetic framework (and the theory behind it) should contribute to the anthropologist's evolutional, ecological and holistic perspectives.

235. List, George. "Fieldwork: Recording Traditional Music." In *Folklore and Folklife: An Introduction,* edited by Richard M. Dorson, 445–454. Chicago: University of Chicago Press, 1972.

Generally introductory in nature, emphasizes interviewing and documentation. Remarks that field collections made by the scholar are, on the whole, of greater value than those made by others. An article on archiving by the same author follows (pp. 455–63).

236. ———. *Music and Poetry in a Colombian Village: A Tri-Cultural Heritage.* Bloomington: Indiana University Press, 1983.

Intensive description and analysis of the *costeños* (inhabitants) of Evitar village, and their music and poetry. Emphasizes the three parent cultures which spawned this music: Spanish-European, African Negro and Amerindian.

237. ———. "Musical Concepts in Traditional Cultures." In *Folklore Today: A Festschrift for Richard M. Dorson*, edited by Linda Dégh et al., 335–46. Bloomington: Indiana University Press, 1976.

Draws upon Hopi *kachina* songs and the music of Colombian *costeños* to identify five categories of responses in the eliciting of musical concepts from informants. An early use of the terms insider (bearer of the tradition) and outsider (scholar-observer) in relation to musical style.

238. Lofland, John. *Analyzing Social Settings: A Guide to Qualitative Observation and Analysis*. The Wadsworth series in Analytical Ethnography. Belmont, Calif.: Wadsworth Publishing Co., 1971. 2nd and abridged ed., 1984.

A field guide written to fill a need in qualitative observation and analysis. Includes explanation of how it differs from quantitative analysis. The 1984 edition differs from the original in that the materials are reordered into a sequence of tasks to be performed in the order they become problematic in research. Several new topics have been added as well as expanded discussions of old topics. Broad sections on gathering, focusing, and analyzing data, and guiding the consequences. Includes a current and comprehensive bibliography. Compare Johnson's *Quantification . . . Research Design* (item 225).

239. McCall, George J. and J. L. Simmons. *Issues in Participant Observation: A Text and Reader*. Addison-Wesley series in Behavioral Science: Quantitative Methods. Reading, Mass.: Addison-Wesley, 1969.

Helps the codification of participant observation procedures by compiling in one volume the complete range of problems and issues, along with the major statements and solutions available in the literature. More than an analytical review of the methodological issues, has usefulness as a source book.

240. Maceda, José. *A Manual of a Field Music Research with Special Reference to Southeast Asia*. Quezon City: UNESCO in cooperation with the Department of Music Research, College of Music, University of the Philippines, 1981.

Mainly applicable for Southeast Asia field studies and Third World researchers. Contains four chapters: A Study of Rural Music in Southeast Asia, Fieldwork, Cataloging, and a Note on Music Transcription. Deals with the techiques and theories of fieldwork but does not cover all the details of music research. Reviewed by Sutton in *EM* 27:140–1.

* SEE ALSO Merriam, Alan. *Anthropology of Music* (item 11).

241. Murphy, Yolanda and Robert F. Murphy. *Women of the Forest.* 2nd ed. New York: Columbia University Press, 1985. Originally published, 1974.

Study of Brazil's Mundurucu Indians, mainly the women. The revision adds a new chapter about the authors' fieldwork from both personal experience and scientific practice.

* SEE ALSO Nettl, Bruno. *Theory and Method in Ethnomusicology* (item 121).

242. Osgood, Charles E. "Semantic Differential Technique in the Comparative Study of Cultures." In *Transcultural Studies in Cognition [report of a conference]*, ed. by A. Kimball Romney and Roy Goodwin D'Andrade. Washington, D.C.: American Anthropological Association, 1964, 171–200. (Special Publication. American Anthropologist, vol. 66, nr. 3, pt. 2).

Author describes his method of research, a theoretical model, for noting differences within languages, how to order them, and the necessity of perceiving certain similarities in the languages as a frame of reference against which to compare them. Illustrates sampling, general procedure.

243. Paredes, Américo. "On Ethnographic Work Among Minority Groups: A Folklorist's Perspective." In *New Directions in Chicano Scholarship*, edited by Ricardo Romo and Raymund Paredes, 1–32. Santa Barbara: UCSB Chicano Studies Center, 1984.

Discusses the special problems in studying Chicano culture that exist between anthropologists and members of the culture itself. Language gets a lot of attention, especially the subtleties of a situation in which the informant is "putting on" the researcher. Advocates a performance-oriented approach to verbal art in the sense of the researcher seeing an informant as engaged in a creative art. An excellent and thought-provoking source about fieldwork which, although directed towards Chicano studies, has a much broader applicability.

244. ———— and Ellen J. Stekert, eds. *The Urban Experience and Folk Tradition*. Publications of the American Folklore Society. Bibliographical and Special Series; v. 22. Austin: University of Texas Press, 1971. o.p.

Provides new approaches to the study of tradition in an urban environment. Illustrates how knowledge of the traditions of rural migrants proves helpful in understanding the currents of modern urban life. Both old and new city folklore are studied. Essays by Dorson, Abrahams, Stekert, Wilgus and Leeds. A special bibliography with preliminary essay is included, pp. 181–200.

245. Payne, Stanley Le Baron. *The Art of Asking Questions*. Studies in Public Opinion, no. 3. 1951. Reprint. Princeton: Princeton University Press, 1980.

Focuses on the wording of single questions almost exclusively, but hardly touches upon problems of question sequence or the overall matter of questionnaire design. Includes a checklist of one hundred considerations.

246. Peacock, James L. *Rites of Modernization: Symbolic and Social Aspects of Indonesian Proletarian Drama*. Symbolic Anthropology series. Chicago: University of Chicago, Press, 1968. Reprint with a new afterword, 1987.

Using *ludruk*, a secular Indonesian drama, as performed in the modern port city of Surabaya, author provides an anthropological model for studying performance and symbolic action. Performances are confronted as totalities. Describes his method for collecting primary data (onstage action, audience responses, language), as well as data on secondary aspects and on the social life of participants. Appendix C, "The Field Research," is especially valuable.

247. Pelto, Pertti J. and Gretel H. Pelto. *Anthropological Research: the Structure of Inquiry*. 2nd ed. Cambridge: Cambridge University Press, 1978.

A basic text that focuses on the essential elements of preparing and manipulating the supporting evidence from which generalizations about human behavior are derived. Concerns the basic principles of research methodology.

248. ———. "Ethnography: The Fieldwork Enterprise." In *Handbook of Social and Cultural Anthropology*, ed. by John J. Honigmann, 241–88. Chicago: Rand McNally, 1973.

Describes one of the first field guides from a historical perspective for ethnographers. Includes "Trends in Contemporary Ethnographic Work," pp. 279–81, and a postlog about "The Future of Ethnographic Work: Problems of Ethics and Relevance," pp. 281–5.

249. Peña, Manuel H. "Ritual Structure in a Chicano Dance." *Latin American Music Review* 1/1 (Spring/Summer 1980):47–73.

Formulates an interpretation, by way of reconstructing the events, of a set of behavioral responses of a Chicano group in Fresno, California, as it participated in Saturday night dances. Result of ten years' experience (1967–77) as a participant-observer. Analysis illuminates the complexities (conflict of values and ideologies) that mark the lives of Mexicans in the U.S. It suggests that a microcosm of this conflict is symbolically played out and ultimately mediated in the ritualized structure of these musical occasions.

250. Phillips, Bernard S. *Social Research: Strategy and Tactics*. 3rd ed. New York: Macmillan, 1976.

Part I is an introduction to scientific method, part II defines the problem (centers on the context of discovery), part III discusses measurement and data construction, part IV analysis and interpretation of data, and part V scientific communication (the results of verification must be communicated in order to provide the basis for further discoveries). Illustrates with data collected during the first two years of a study on recruiting medical students into a career in public health. Both theoretical and methodological. Third edition is aimed at the more humanistic scientist.

251. Powdermaker, Hortense. *Stranger and Friend: The Way of an Anthropologist*. New York: Norton, 1966. London: Secher and Warburg, 1967.

Author covers four major field research experiences in detail: 1) a late Stone-Age Melanesian society in the Southwest Pacific (1929–30); 2) a rural Mississippi community—half Negro and half White (1933–34); 3) Hollywood (1946–47); and 4) an African mining township in Northern Rhodesia (1953–54). In recounting her field studies she looks inward as well as outward, with benefit of hindsight, and concludes that the effective fieldworker learns about himself as well as about the people he studies. Lists honesty and accuracy as of primary importance. Discusses participant observation.

252. Rosaldo, Renato. *The Culture of Truth: the Remaking of Social Analysis*. Boston: Beacon Press, 1989.

An important work that casts doubt on the notion of objectivity and science in humanistic research such as anthropology. Argues that a change in cultural studies has eroded once-dominant conceptions of truth and objectivity. The truth of objectivism competes with the truths of case studies that are embedded in local contexts, shaped by local interests, and colored by local perceptions.

253. Rouch, Jean. "The Camera and Man." *Studies in the Anthropology of Visual Communication* 1/1 (1974):37–44.

One of the four articles translated by Steve Feld and mentioned in Feld's "Avant Propos: Jean Rouch." Mainly concerned with the history and theory of anthropology film, Rouch summarizes the experiments and trends that have taken place since 1960. Concludes it has not yet passed the experimental stage [it is 1974]. Outlines his belief in a "shared cine-anthropology."

254. Royce, Anya Peterson. *The Anthropology of Dance*. Midland Book edition. Bloomington: Indiana University Press, 1980, c1977.

Author describes herself as an anthropologist concerned with human behavior. Writes about the integration of individuals and culture, and the impossibility of taking dance out of its proper context as an aspect of human behavior. Of particular interest is chapter 3 (pp. 38–63), where her purpose is to remove some of the mystery surrounding the dance and to suggest practical means for lessening the difficulties of collecting dance data. She describes and discusses various notations for talking about dance, mainly Laban and Benesh, but points out their limitations for notating in the field. Recommends films of dance as well as field guides.

255. Rynkiewich, Michael A. and James P. Spradley, eds. *Ethics and Anthropology: Dilemmas in Fieldwork*. New York: Wiley, 1976. Reprint ed. Malabar, Fla.: R. E. Krieger Publishing Co., 1981.

Collection of case studies which explore the ethical dimension of anthropology at the grass roots level. First-person accounts by anthropologists on a dilemma or series of problems involving personal values and beliefs. Context is described, conflicting choices faced by the author, the people involved, the emotions and doubts that emerged, and the partially satisfactory results and resolutions. Includes an appendix, "Principles of professional responsibility adopted by the Council of the American Anthropological Association, May, 1971."

256. Schatzman, Leonard and Anselm Strauss. *Field Research: Strategies for a Natural Sociology*. Prentice-Hall Methods of Social Science series. Englewood Cliffs, N.J.: Prentice-Hall, 1973.

Describes a mode of research and links its operations to the social psychology of the researcher, to the social situations in which he finds himself, and to the logic of the inquiry in which he is engaged. Recommended are the chapters on logic and social psychology of social research, the various strategy chapters (for entering, for getting started, for watching, for listening, for analysis, for recording, and for communicating research). Emphasis is on the researcher himself/herself.

257. Seeger, Anthony. *Nature and Society in Central Brazil: The Suyá Indians of Mato Grosso.* Harvard Studies in Cultural Anthropology, 4. Cambridge: Harvard University Press, 1981.

Difficulties of getting fieldwork started are detailed in a situation where researcher had to wait eight months before gaining permission to go into the field. Book covers such aspects as Suyá cosmology, classification of animals and plants by odor, principles of kinship and naming, and the process of the life cycle. Lacks discussion of music (it comes in his later work, see item 164).

258. Shelemay, Kay Kaufman. "Together in the Field: Team Research Among Syrian Jews in Brooklyn, New York." *Ethnomusicology* 32/3 (Fall 1988):369–84.

Describes team research project, research design and evaluation, as well as implications for her own future research. Unexpected benefit was the value of the project to the group being studied.

259. Smith, Barbara B. "Indigenous and Non-Indigenous Researchers. Implications for Content and Method in the Study of Music in Oceania." In *Report of the Twelfth Congress, Berkeley 1977* [of the International Musicological Society], 132–33. Kassel: Bärenreiter, 1981.

In a conference session titled "Music of Oceania," the author points to a relatively new phenomenon whereby indigenous researchers (cultural insiders) research their own music. Governments are also allocating funds for this. Identification of six trends is followed by a discussion.

260. Spindler, George Dearborn, ed. *Being an Anthropologist: Fieldwork in Eleven Cultures.* Reissued with changes. Prospect Heights, Ill.: Waveland Press, 1986. Originally published by New York: Holt, Rinehard and Winston, 1970.

A report of how thirteen anthropologists made an adaptation [to someone else's way of life as well as adoption of the other's point of view] in eleven different cultures. Very personal reporting although methods of data collection and analysis are discussed as well. Editor hopes that the case studies help to humanize one of the fundamental tasks of anthropology. The reissue has a new introduction, "In Retrospect and Prospect: 1986." Remarks on the changes in anthropology since 1970, especially the criticisms leveled by younger scholars against older works. Feeling that anthropology is not the objective exercise in positivistic social science that it once was, defends the "out there" rather than "in here" view of cultural data.

261. Spradley, James P., ed. *Culture and Cognition: Rules, Maps, and Plans*. Chandler Publications in Anthropology and Sociology. San Francisco: Chandler Publishing Co., 1972; Prospect Heights, Ill.: Waveland Press, 1987.

Compares the routine of his student days (or rather, the nights) working in an egg company with life in human society where behavior is organized on the basis of a shared symbolic world. Identifies the theme of his book as the nature of shared cognition or cultural knowledge. Chapter on "Foundations of cultural knowledge" is particularly recommended (pp. 3–38).

262. ———. *The Ethnographic Interview*. New York: Holt, Rinehart and Winston, 1979.

Systematic handbook for undertaking ethnography. Companion volume to *Participant Observation* (item 263). Designed both for students and professionals trying to learn the skills of ethnography. Develops the idea of sequenced tasks. Chapters divided into two parts: 1) ethnographic research, and 2) the developmental research sequence.

263. ———. *Participant Observation*. New York: Holt, Rinehart and Winston, 1980.

How to do fieldwork using the method of participant observation with step-by-step instructions. Promotes carrying out of tasks in a logical sequence. Part 1 is on ethnography and culture, Part 2 on the developmental research sequence.

264. ——— and David W. McCurdy. *The Cultural Experience: Ethnography in Complex Society*. Chicago: Science Research Associates, 1972. Paperback reprint, Waveland Press, 1988.

Undergraduate textbook that advocates an approach to ethnography by describing a culture in its own terms (New Ethnography or Ethnographic Semantics). Chapters are organized according to the basic steps and difficulties that make up the research process; the chapter on fieldwork is particularly recommended.

265. Stone, Ruth M. and Verlon L. Stone. "Event, Feedback, and Analysis: Research Media in the Study of Music Events." *Ethnomusicology* 25/2 (May 1981):215–25.

Examines 1) the use of technological media for studying the music event, and 2) the feedback interview as a research technique. Feedback interview is defined as the playback and recall of a completed event in which the researcher and participant attempt to reconstruct the event's meaning. The human being is considered both as a unique kind of medium and as the operator and interpreter of all other mediating agencies. Consults participants to determine what meanings they construct. Offers possibilities for studying process in the making of music, grounding the study in empiric reality, and accounting for meaning from various perspectives.

266. Titon, Jeff Todd. "Stance, Role and Identity in Fieldwork among Folk Baptists and Pentecostals." *American Music* 3/1 (Spring 1985):16–24.

Critical of Herndon and McLeod, and of Jos Koning's methods, author largely explores the total picture of fieldwork involvement.

267. Turner, Victor W. and Edward M. Bruner, eds. *The Anthropology of Experience.* Urbana: University of Illinois Press, 1986.

Essays from a 1980 symposium formulated by Turner, who in turn was inspired by Dilthey's theory of hermeneutics and the interpretation of cultural expression through experience. Following an introductory essay by Bruner, papers by Turner, Abrahams, F. Turner, R. Rosaldo, Bruner, Fernandez, Kapferer, Gorfain, Boon, Myerhoff, Stewart, Babcock, Schechner and Geertz develop and elaborate different aspects of the theme.

268. Wachsmann, Klaus. "The Changeability of Musical Experience."
      Ethnomusicology 26/2 (May 1982):197–215.

      Draws on his personal conversations with Charles Seeger on
      topics such as the meaning of music, and from his own musical
      experiences (listening to his first recording of Cameroons music on
      an old cylinder, his Uganda years, as a violinist in a string quartet).
      The Seeger distinguished lecture, 1981 S.E.M. conference.

269. Wax, Rosalie H. *Doing Fieldwork: Warnings and Advice*. 1971.
      Reprint. Chicago: University of Chicago Press, 1986.

      Description of her personal experiences in three field locations:
      Japanese-American relocation centers in 1943–45; fieldwork on
      Thrashing Buffalo Reservation, 1962–63; and Six Friendly Tribes,
      1966–67. Introductory chapters cover theoretical presuppositions of
      fieldwork, the first and most uncomfortable stage, a historical
      sketch, and the ambiguities of fieldwork.

270. Whitehead, Tony Larry and Mary Ellen Conaway. *Self, Sex and
      Gender in Cross-Cultural Fieldwork*. Champaign, Ill.: University
      of Illinois Press, 1986.

      On the systematic relationship between the experience of
      cross-cultural fieldwork *and* the fieldworkers' sense of gender and
      self. Addresses the feedback process in the relationship between the
      fieldworker and the field community, that is, the impact of the
      personality and actions of the fieldworker on the field community
      which in turn works in reverse. Chapters written by different
      authors.

271. Whyte, William Foote. *Street Corner Society; the Social Structure
      of an Italian Slum*. 3rd rev. ed. Chicago: University of Chicago
      Press, 1981.

      Details the author's research methods, including how he lived
      during the period of study. Appendix A, On the evolution of the
      book, *Street Corner Society* (pp. 279–358) is especially valuable.

272. Williams, Thomas Rhys. *Field Methods in the Study of Culture.* Studies in Anthropological Method. New York: Holt, Rinehart and Winston, [1967].

    Covers a wide range of the methods used by anthropologists in the study of culture. Author's research experience in Duisan communities (N. Borneo) is used for illustration.

273. Zemp, Hugo. "Filming Music and Looking at Music Films." *Ethnomusicology* 32/3 (Fall, 1988):393–427.

    Discusses filming in relation to fieldwork, with technical advice on camera angles and editing, as well as the personal philosophy of the author.

IV. MUSICAL ANALYSIS

274. Adams, Charles T. "Melodic Contour Typology." *Ethnomusicology* 20/2 (May 1976):179–215.

A review of the basic approaches and assumptions in melodic contour description and typology. Proposes a specific formal definition and a typology that differentiates melodic type and shape; explores also the productiveness of the proposed typology and its constituent features in a comparative analysis of Flathead and Paiute Indian songs.

275. Beaudry, Nicole. "Toward Transcription and Analysis of Inuit Throat-Games: Macro-Structure." *Ethnomusicology* 22/2 (May 1978):261–73.

Concerns voicing and breathing techniques. Methodology involves a four-step discovery process of expanding perceptions, transcriptions, and analysis. Reveals four basic types of vocal production and their variable usage, and that the macro-structure falls within specific parameters: 1) texts comprising morphones and vocables, 2) fixed and relative pitches, 3) ternary and binary rhythmic elements, 4) voicing and respiration dichotomies in vocal-tract activity, 5) accentuation, pitch, continuity, dynamics, timbre, and 6) formation rules for the selection, presentation, and repetition of motives. Companion article to Charron's (item 280) on micro structure, using a semiotic approach.

276. Bengtsson, Ingmar. "On Melody Registration and 'Mona.'" *Elektronische Datenverarbeitung in der Musikwissenschaft*, ed. by Harald Heckmann, 136–74. Regensburg: Gustav Bosse, 1967.

A clear explanation of the Swedish transcription aid for monophony termed "Mona," designed by physicians at Uppsala University for the Institute of Musicology. Discusses some theoretical and terminological problems connected with the use of different so-called "objective" methods of registration employed in musicology. In addition, some aspects of the practical exploitation of such recordings is touched upon. At the time of writing, a twin project "Polly," for the analysis of more complex sound events (multi-part music), was in the planning phase.

277. Berry, Wallace. *Form in Music.* Englewood Cliffs: Prentice-Hall, 1966. 2nd ed. 1986.

As with LaRue (item 403), this text is intended for the analysis of Western classical music. However, it provides some helpful structural principles that can also be applied to the analysis of non-Western music.

278. Boilès, Charles. "Reconstruction of Proto-Melody." *Yearbook for Inter-American Musical Research* 9 (1973):45–63.

Introduces a comparative method for studying song forms found in Western cultures. A glimpse into the past affords the opportunity to observe how notes were added or dropped, and how durational values and pitches were altered. Follows the process of musical diffusion and traces an extant melody in a given world area to its parent form elsewhere. Uses eleven cognate versions of the Spanish *romance* "Don Gato," to demonstrate.

279. Burman-Hall, Linda C. "Southern American Folk Fiddle Styles." *Ethnomusicology* 19/1 (Jan. 1975):47–65.

Purpose is to establish the widespread characteristics of British-American traditional instrumental music as preserved in the primary form of fiddle music, and to define the principal regional substyles of fiddle tradition in the Southern states. Creates a frame of reference by which this tradition may be readily contrasted with similar instrumental styles and a basis upon which hybrid folk and commercially successful descendants of traditional fiddling may be evaluated stylistically. A revised portion of author's doctoral dissertation.

280. Charron, Claude. "Toward Transcription and Analysis of Inuit Throat-Games: Micro-Structure." *Ethnomusicology* 22/2 (May 1978):245–59.

Companion article to Beaudry's (item 275) on macro structure using a semiotic approach. Considers two different aspects of the material: intonation contours and contrasts of voiced versus voiceless pitch. Uses sonograms and mingograms to help analyze patterns articulated in a vocal production.

281. Chenoweth, Vida. *Melodic Perception and Analysis: a Manual on Ethnic Melody.* Papua, New Guinea: Summer Institute of Linguistics, 1971.

As a textbook for the analysis of ethnic melody, reviews the analytical techniques taught in the classroom to aid the fieldworker. Author divides the work into four parts: prologue, etic and emic elements, grammar of music, and semantics of music. Some of part 1 has to do with preparation, equipment and identification of tapes. Critically reviewed by Marcia Herndon (*EM* 18/2:303–4).

282. ——— and Darlene Bee. "Comparative-Generative Models of a New Guinea Melodic Structure." *American Anthropologist* 73 (1971):773–82.

Using a New Guinea music system for illustration, utilizes three methods of melodic description: 1) the flow diagram, 2) formulas, and 3) a geometric model. Proposes these as useful tools in the areas of melodic description, comparison of musical styles or systems, and composing in a given ethnic style or system.

283. Cohen, Dalia and Ruth Katz. "The Interdependence of Notation Systems and Musical Information." *Yearbook of the International Folk Music Council* 11, 1979 (1979):100–13.

Concerns the relationship between various means and methods, and the varied aims of notation and preservation. Kinds of musical preservation are charted in such a way as to reveal the interdependence between the oral and written parts, the complexity of style, and the pace of change.

284. ———. "Remarks Concerning the Use of the Melograph in Ethnomusicological Studies." *Yuval* 1 (1968):155–68.

Discusses the operation of the Israeli Melograph, the problems raised by the new musical material it provides, and the methods of research it suggests. Points to areas of investigation that have been overlooked. Examples used are one Arab and one Hebrew song. The tonal skeleton, as determined by analysis of scatter patterns, characterizes not only the melody and melody-type (*maqam*) but also yields a definition of cultural particularity.

285. Durbin, Mridula Adenwala. "Transformational Models Applied to Musical Analysis: Theoretical Possibilities." *Ethnomusicology* 15/3 (Sept. 1971):353–62.

Attempt by an anthropologist to indicate the parameters of three phenomena—normal speech, poetry, and song text—in terms of a single method of model-making derived from Chomskian linguistic analysis.

286. Ellis, Catherine J. "The Role of the Ethnomusicologist in the Study of Andagarinja Women's Ceremonies." *Miscellanea Musicologica* (Adelaide) 5 (1970):76–208.

Comprehensive study of an Andagarinja women's ceremony. Discusses one particular recording within the context of the whole collection, within the framework of the various types of collecting, and the specific problems to be overcome in collecting and analysis. Describes the most effective approach the ethnomusicologist can adopt in studying a rapidly disintegrating musical tradition. Shows that the structure of the songs is not random. Specific musical techniques are shown as communication devices within the framework of a ceremony. Comments freely on the difficulties as well as advantages of team research in the field.

287. England, Nicholas M. "Symposium on Transcription and Analysis: A Hukwe Song with Musical Bow." *Ethnomusicology* 8/3 (Sept. 1964):223–77.

From a symposium organized by England and presented during the 1963 meeting of S.E.M. at Wesleyan University.

Participants were Robert Garfias, Mieczyslaw Kolinski, George List and Willard Rhodes; moderator and chairman was Charles Seeger. Each participant came with his prepared transcription. Aim was to provide material for thought to everyone interested in transcription. A symposium often referred to in the literature on analysis and transcription. One of the first examples of analysis with an accompanying recording, a 7" disc of the musical example discussed: "Hukwe Song with Musical Bow" recorded by England, Peabody-Harvard Kalahari Expedition (1959) in South-West Africa.

288. Erdely, Stephen and R. A. Chipman. "Strip-Chart Recordings of Narrow Band Frequency Analysis in Aid of Ethnomusicological Data." *Yearbook of the International Folk Music Council* 4, 1972 (1973):119–36.

Aims to elaborate further on the Seeger solution (that the transcription of music will only be accurate when musicians are confronted by an objective analysis of sound waves). Uses the output of a Sound and Vibration Analyzer with the 1/3 octave bandwidth selector, fed into a General Radio Type Frequency Meter and Discriminator. Output signal from the integrator drives one channel of a Dual Channel DC amplifier and recorder (a strip-chart recorder). Four songs used to illustrate: two Irish (a pipe tune and a popular tune) and two Hungarian (a folk song and a popular tune). Investigation showed more than bringing musical notation and strip-chart recording into correlation, e.g., frequency readings from fast tempo tunes and rubato passages.

289. Herndon, Marcia. "Analysis: The Herding of Sacred Cows?" *Ethnomusicology* 18/2 (May 1974):219–62.

Includes a review of the literature on musical analysis as a catalyst for debate. Presents a model derived from set theory and basic scientific method. Uses the musical example of "Zaodahy!," a Malagasy children's first hair-cutting song. See also Kolinski's "Herndon's Verdict . . . " (item 300) and "Final Reply" (item 299) and Herndon's "Reply to Kolinski . . . " (item 290).

290. ———. "Reply to Kolinski: Tarus Omicida." *Ethnomusicology* 20/2 (May 1976):217–31.

In a defense of "sacred cows" article (289), urges Kolinski to clarify his methodology, and rebuts Blum's criticism that she was intending her remarks on other scholars' methods as a parody. Further clarifies her model based on set theory. See also her "Analysis . . . " (item 289) and Kolinski's "Herndon's Verdict . . . " (item 300) and "Final Reply" (item 299).

291. Hopkins, Pandora. "The Purposes of Transcription." *Ethnomusicology* 10/3 (Sept. 1966):310–17.

Uses Hardanger fiddle notation's concept of visual design to illustrate particular aspects of musical design. Considers conventional staff notation as a medium for comparison. Sees the prescriptive role of notation as limited, but the communication of the transcriber's opinion as its primary purpose.

292. Jairazbhoy, Nazir. "Nominal Units of Time: A Counterpart for Ellis' System of Cents." *Selected Reports* 4 (1983):113–24.

Introduces system of measurement and description of time intervals in music where the basic unit is NUT (Nominal Unit of Time). A hundred unit standard parallels Ellis's cent system for pitch. Has two applications: 1) NUT standard applied to any note value deemed to be meaningful in the context being examined; and 2) analyses of the internal subdivisions of a metric time cycle accepted within the culture as consisting of a specific number of time units or pulses. Offers an alternative from cumbersome ratio-based Western notation, although its main contribution may be in the area of performance practice.

293. ———. "The 'Objective' and Subjective View in Music Transcription." *Ethnomusicology* 21/2 (May 1977):263–73.

Examines aspects of recording and transcription. Points out that the basic premises underlying development and use of automatic transcribers has been inadequately explored. Also, there has been no thorough examination of the relevance of an objective look at sound (transcribed by a machine) to ethnomusicological studies. Examines the physiological aspects of hearing, the unconscious working of sound in the brain, and the selectivity of sound as considered by musical conventions of the culture. Automatic transcription cannot be a replacement for aural transcription; they perform different but equally justifiable functions.

294. Katz, Ruth. "Mannerism and Cultural Change: An Ethnomusicological Example." *Current Anthropology* 2/4–5 (1970):465–75.

Based on a systematic analysis of musical materials of three generations of Aleppo Jews in Israel, a theory of the initial stages of one type of culture change is proposed. Central proposition is that the apparent resistance to acceptance of majority group culture may be expressed in "manneristic" terms, i.e., in terms of the exaggeration and embellishment of those elements of traditional culture whereby the majority identifies the minority and the minority comes to identify itself. Suggests that this type of culture change is found particularly in minority groups well-accepted in the overall social structure but nonetheless steadfast in their desire to preserve some of their traditional forms. "Mannerism" is used to denote the tension between conflicting stylistic elements and to signal the decline of a style.

295. Kauffman, Robert. "African Rhythm: A Reassessment." *Ethnomusicology* 24/3 (Sept. 1980):393–415.

Concentrates on the nature of music making, including rhythm, of particular peoples within the continent of Africa. A similarity or unity is apparent, also having to do with African influences upon Black music in the Americas. Briefly describes current theories of African rhythm. Notes especially the macrorhythmic level: the rhythmic aspects of language, the nature of multichronometry in dance, the identification of a density referent and multilineal relationships at the microrhythmic level, and more precise determination of the nature of multipart relationships.

296. Knopoff, Leon. "Some Technological Advances in Musical Analysis." *Studia Musicologica* 7 (1965):301–7.

  Summarizes three new developments in the field of electro-mechanical instruments pertinent to some problems of musical recording and analysis: 1) recording and notating a piece played on several percussion instruments using time-sequence recorders (strip-chart recorders); 2) a device to record an index for the instrumental quality of an instrument producing a sustained tone (his own construction); and 3) a quantitative scheme to determine the rhythmic content of a given piece (Melograph Model B).

297. Koetting, James. "Analysis and Notation of West African Drum Ensemble Music." *Selected Reports* (Los Angeles: U.C.L.A. Institute of Ethnomusicology) 1/3 (1970):116–46.

  Emphasis on analysis of the music in its own structural terms. Important in the introduction of T.U.B.S. (Time Unit Box System) notation developed by the author as a more adequate aid to the analysis of drum ensemble music.

298. Kolinski, Mieczyslaw. "Classification of Tonal Structures." *Studies in Ethnomusicology* 1 (1961):38–76. [o.p.]

  Designed to facilitate descriptive and comparative research on the tonal construction of tribal, Eastern and Western music. Concerns the acoustical relationships between notes employed in a tonal pattern. Author develops his ideas on "tint" (the specifically musical quality of sounds that is identical in octave tones and more or less dissimilar in other tone relations). A comparative chart of tints (pp. 44–71) of American Indian, African Negro, Afro-American and English-American structures, makes up a large part of the article.

299. ———. "Final Reply to Herndon." *Ethnomusicology* 21/1 (Jan. 1977):75–83.

  Concludes that the exchange of views between Herndon and himself will have benefitted the discussion of problems in the field of study. See Herndon's "Analysis . . . " (item 289) and "Reply to

Kolinski" (item 290) and Kolinski's "Herndon's Verdict" (item 300).

300. ———. "Herndon's Verdict on Analysis: *Tabula rasa.*" *Ethnomusicology* 20/1 (Jan. 1976):1–22.

Rebuts Herndon's criticisms of his general concepts, mainly "scale formula," tempo figures, recurrent movement of melodic construction, and "tint." Applies his method to the same Malagasy "Zaodahy" song as Herndon. See also Kolinski's "Final Reply . . . " (item 299) and Herndon's "Analysis . . . " (item 289) and "Reply to Kolinski" (item 290).

301. List, George. "The Musical Significance of Transcription." *Ethnomusicology* 7/3 (Sept. 1963):193–7.

Comments on Hood's paper on "Musical Significance," primarily the application of a musicological approach to ethnomusicology through notation and transcription. Concerns in particular transcription and analysis in the context of the culture of which the music is a part. Reviews why transcription is necessary or has value (for comparison), the advantages and disadvantages of the human ear, and of electronic devices.

302. ———. "The Reliability of Transcription." *Ethnomusicology* 18/3 (Sept. 1974):353–77. Accompanying "soundsheet" recording.

From his seminar on transcription List and his students analyze and discuss three different musical examples: a Romanian *colinda* (carol), a Yiddish lullaby, and a Thai lullaby. Concludes that transcriptions made by ear are sufficiently accurate and reliable to provide a valid basis for analysis and comparative studies of two aspects of music style, pitch and duration.

303. McLean, Mervyn. "An Analysis of 651 Maori Scales." *Yearbook of the International Folk Music Council* 1 (1971):123–64.

Three scales (and a possible fourth) were derived from interval associations using strict criteria for melodic usage. These coincide with plagal forms of the medieval Phrygian, Ionian, and Aeolian modes. Concludes that there is no explanation for these parallels between Maori scales and those of medieval Europe and ancient Greece.

304. McLeod, Norma. "Some Techniques of Analysis for Non-Western Music." Ph.D. diss. (anthropology), Northwestern University, 1966.

Establishes an approach to musical analysis which allows music to be described as a Gestalt. Requires that the various types of sound which combine in its basic structure be described both separately and together.

305. Manuel, Peter. "Modal Harmony in Andalusian, Eastern, and Turkish Syncretic Musics." *Yearbook for Traditional Music* 21 (1989):70–94.

Examines the standardized ways of harmonizing predominantly modal melodies in the contexts of a set of interrelated urban folk and popular musics of the Mediterranean area that employ a harmonic-melodic system qualitatively distinct from that of Western practice. Seeks to revive the spirit of "comparative musicology" and to suggest ways in which cross-cultural comparison of selected musical parameters may reveal new sorts of pan-regional music areas. Considers "Mediterranean tonality" a form of modal harmony (combining aspects of "modal polyphony" and "chordal harmony"). Shows that urban Arab music has, for the most part, not assimilated this tonality. Hopes that this article will inspire further research into broader aspects as well as details of the use of chordal harmony in the regions discussed.

306. Nattiez, Jean-Jacques. "Is a Descriptive Semiotics of Music Possible?" *Language Sciences* 23 (Dec. 1972):1–7.

Concludes that the notion of transformation has different meanings in linguistics and in the semiotics of music; its fields of application are not the same. One essential characteristic is retained, that of describing explicitly the passing from one phrase or sequence to another. This can lead to the formalized semiotics of musical styles and systems.

307. ———. "Linguistics: A New Approach for Musical Analysis?" *International Review of the Aesthetics and Sociology of Music* 4/1 (1973):51–68.

Musical semiology can be defined as a science which employs linguistic models to analyze musical works. The states of linguistics and musical analysis are compared. Problems of musical analysis are examined from four points of view: 1) how the object of musical analysis is defined, 2) the procedures of the analysis, 3) the metalanguage used in musical analysis, and 4) the procedures of validation of the models.

308. Powers, Harold S. "Language Models and Musical Analysis." *Ethnomusicology* 24/1 (Jan. 1980):1–60.

Urges that in applications of the music-as-language metaphor, attention should be paid to diverse musical traditions in musical terms, not only traditions of the musics we study but also traditions of *how* we study music. Analytical theorists of Western music can profit from reflecting on theories and studies of other musical practices. Language models for musical analysis used circumspectly can contribute fundamentally to musical disciplines.

309. ———. "Mode." *The New Grove Dictionary of Music and Musicians* 12 (1980):376–450.

Especially part IV, "Modal Scales and Folksong Melodies," and part V, "Mode as a Musicological Concept," do much to expand and internationalize the concept of mode in music. *Maqam, raga, patet,* and *chosi* are discussed at some length both individually and comparatively. A helpful bibliography completes this substantial article.

310. Qureshi, Regula Burckhardt. "Musical Sound and Contextual Input: A Performance Model for Musical Analysis." *Ethnomusicology* 31/1 (Winter 1987):56–86.

Isolates an analytical model from the study of *qawwali*, the music of the Sufi assembly of India and Pakistan. Primary focus is on the musical sound idiom, thus incorporating a musicological focus into an anthropological paradigm. Two kinds of tools are identified as useful, one concerning the musical sound system, and the other concerning the analysis of the performance context. Argues, however, for a truly ethnomusicological approach, and encourages others to review her conclusions and model in a wider musical context. She believes her approach may provide a means of explaining how musical systems are used in performance on the basis of contextual meaning.

311. Rahn, Jay. *A Theory for All Musics: Problems and Solutions in the Analysis of Non-Western Forms.* Toronto: University of Toronto Press, 1983.

Attempts to build on Benjamin Boretz's "Meta-variations" essays and to expand its base of application from Western music to a broad range of the musics of the world. Applies his method to a Sweathouse song of the Flathead, the 'Du' Hukwe bow song, Asaadua of the Akan, Lin Yu's music for the Confucian temple, and the hornpipes in Harding's Collection. Some consider his treatment of three aspects of musical culture (values, concepts, and norms) as a theoretical research model (see item 110). Critically reviewed by Richard I. Cohn (*EM* 32:149–52).

312. Seeger, Charles. "Versions and Variants of the Tunes of 'Barbara Allen.'" *Selected Reports in Ethnomusicology* 1/1 (1966):120–67.

This most widely known of all Child ballads in the U.S. illustrates the problem of identifying a ballad tune. Author uses 76 recorded examples from the Library of Congress. Describes the ordering and classification of the songs to facilitate their study. In melodic contour two versions were identified; words remained the same. Melograph Model B was used to assist in one version. Concludes that there is no such entity as *the* Barbara Allen tune. "Comment on the Words" by Ed Cray reveal four basic text versions.

313. *Selected Reports in Ethnomusicology* 2/1 (Los Angeles: University of California, 1974). Guest editor: Peter Crossley-Holland.

Contains twelve essays using the Seeger Melograph as a transcription aid. Developed during a seminar in 1970 at U.C.L.A.'s Department of Music. Contains an introductory article on the Melograph Model C by Michael Moore, technician. Other articles are grouped in two sections: those on the human voice (Alice Moyle, Jozef Pacholczyk, Margaret Caton, Ronald Walcott, Marjory Liu, and David Morton), and those on selected musical instruments (Craig Woodson, Don Addison, Reis Flora, Ray Giles, and Thomas Owens).

314. Tove, P. A., B. Norman, L. Isaksson and J. Czekajewski. "A Direct-Recording Frequency and Amplitude Meter for Analysis of Musical and Other Sonic Waveforms." *Journal of the Acoustical Society of America* 39/2 (1966):362–71.

Concerns the objective notation of musical melodies, and of frequency and time relations in the study of musical phenomena produced by single unisonous instruments or song. The possibility of extracting the fundamental pitch and measuring and recording it is described together with the transistorized instrument performing this function. It is a technical description of the Uppsala machine called "Mona," a distant cousin of the Norwegian "melody-writer" developed by Gurvin in Oslo in the 50s, and of the somewhat less distant relation to Seeger's various Melographs.

315. Vaughn, Kathryn. "Exploring Emotion in Sub-Structural Aspects of Karelian Lament: Application of Time Series Analysis to Digitized Melody." *Yearbook for Traditional Music* 22 (1990):106–22.

An application of the computer directed to the performance itself. Proposes that a melodic contour be viewed as an analog of musical behavior and that it, therefore, comprises a map of at least one parameter which may be studied for the purposes of qualitative interpretation of music in culture. Uses as her data base the Karelian laments recorded by Tolbert (item 186). Uses a time series analysis defined as any sequence of measurements made over a given period of time. Paper is based on the hypothesis that the singer's vibrato gives cues regarding musical emotion.

316. Waterhouse, David. "Towards a New Analysis of Rhythm in Music." In *Cross-Cultural Perspectives*, edited by Robert Falck

and Timothy Rice, 29–37 (Toronto: University of Toronto Press, 1982).

Motivation for the article arises from the author's belief that there are grave shortcomings in the literature on rhythm. Advocates the serious analysis of rhythm-in-performance, and proposes an informal structural model for it.

V. SOURCES FROM RELATED FIELDS

317. Abrahams, Roger D. "Toward an Enactment-Centered Theory of Folklore." In *Frontiers of Folklore*, edited by William R. Bascom, 79–120. AAAS Selected Symposium, 5. Boulder: Westview Press, [1977]. [o.p.]

    Defines enactment as a term that includes any cultural event in which community members come together to participate, e.g., performances, games, rituals, festivities. Enactments stylize and epitomize the everyday. A critical methodology is needed to enable the researcher to describe behavior patterns within one culture as well as to compare them cross-culturally. Looks at play and compares it with ritual. Searches expressive interaction for ways to understand and interpret the less stylized and self-conscious stream of life. Feels a theory of enactment must describe what is unique about each realm of man's capacity to coordinate and intensify his behavior; at the same time it must demonstrate how such an intensification of life provides a frame of reference by which the less intensive, the more random and spontaneous may be better understood.

318. Abu-Lughod, Lila. "Honor and the Sentiments of Loss in a Bedouin Society." *American Ethnologist* 12/2 (1985):245–61.

    Explores the significance of coexisiting, discrepant discourses on emotion in order to grasp the relationship between the self and the cultural ideal. Represents the application of performance theory, particularly in dealing with emotion.

319. ———. *Veiled Sentiments: Honor and Poetry in a Bedouin Society*. Berkeley: University of California Press, 1987, 1986.

    Personal story of a half-Egyptian, half-American researcher who lived in an Awlad' Ali household in the Western desert of

Egypt as an adopted daughter. Identifies with contextual or performance-oriented studies of oral literature, particularly those which focus on the individual and the social situation of recitations, the uses to which recitations are put in social interactions, and the creativity involved in manipulating traditional forms such as songs, proverbs and folktales.

320. Adorno, Theodor W. *Introduction to the Sociology of Music.* Translated by E. B. Ashton. New York: Seabury, 1968. Reprint. New York: Continuum, 1976.

Author is the chief representative of a sociology of music based on historical idealism. His ideas were introduced (and assembled in this book) in the early sixties during a lecture series at Frankfurt University. Believes that the differentiation of musical material in a composition is a relatively independent gauge of the level of the social awareness reflected in it. His criterion for judging this is the inner coherence of musical structure (which in light music, for example, is absent).

321. Armstrong, Robert Plant. *The Powers of Presence: Consciousness, Myth and Affecting Presence.* Philadelphia: University of Pennsylvania Press, 1981.

Continues developing two ideas from previous works, *The Affecting Presence* and *Wellspring*: that the work of "art" is a presence, and that it abides in power. Particularly addresses the previously unquestioned ethnocentric assumption that all works of art are everywhere endowed with the same "aesthetic" properties and that these relate to "beauty" and "virtuosity." When considering non-Western cultures, these presumptions are radically challenged. Represents the influence of performance theory, particularly emotion.

322. Auerbach, Susan. "From Singing to Lamenting: Women's Musical Role in a Greek Village." In *Women and Music in Cross-Cultural Perspective*, ed. by Ellen Koskoff, 25–43. New York: Greenwood Press, 1987. Reprint. Urbana, Ill.: University of Illinois Press, 1989.

Traces the passage from singing to lamenting that characterizes the musical experience of women over fifty in the Epirot village of Kalohori. Field data on indigenous concepts of gender and music, observation of village musical behavior, and anthropological sources on women and mourning are the basis for three related questions. Why and how is women's singing constrained and their lamenting encouraged in village culture? What is the significance of the song-lament passage for older women song carriers and the music system in general? How do women function within their assigned roles to fulfill individual expressive needs? Author aims to account for Greek women's songs and laments as socially meaningful expressions tied to gender identity.

323. Babcock, Barbara. *The Reversible World: Symbolic Inversion in Art and Society.* Symbol, Myth and Ritual series. Ithaca: Cornell University Press, 1978. [o.p.]

Representative of a school of British social anthropology as well as of symbolic anthropology, this collection of symposium papers treats the concept of symbolic inversion or reversal. Older than the term itself, the concept is central to literary notions of irony, parody, and paradox, i.e., the world upside down. First five essays deal primarily with processes of inversion particular to Western art and literature, the second five essays with reversals in action, that is, on the ritual and social uses of inverted images. Papers from Forms of Symbolic Inversion Symposium, Toronto, 1972.

324. Barnett, Steve. "Identity Choice and Caste Ideology in Contemporary South India." In *Symbolic Anthropology; a Reader in the Study of Symbols and Meanings*, edited by J. Dolgin et al., 270–91. New York: Columbia University Press, 1977.

Considers the character of social change in India to illustrate a powerful generalized model of how ideological forms are created or transformed and how they are generative in and of social action. Represents a link between performance theory, Lévi-Strauss and structuralism.

325. Basso, Ellen B. *A Musical View of the Universe: Kalapalo Myth and Ritual Performances*. University of Pennsylvania Publications in Conduct and Communication series. Philadelphia: University of Pennsylvania Press, 1985.

Collection of myths from a central Brazilian people who use music ritually as a means of communicating between what they define as insurmountably separated or grossly unequal categories of beings. A strong parallel between their ideas of language and of music. A. Seeger has remarked that the author stresses a unified approach to performance genres through the symbolism of sound production (Seeger 1987:xv). Robertson reviews it as a contribution to the domain of ethnographic understanding as well as to performance practice (*EM* 33:549–51).

326. Bauman, Richard. "Performance and Honor in 13th Century Iceland." *Journal of American Folklore* 99 (1986):131–50.

Employing the poetics of performance, analyzes the interrelationships between artistic verbal performance and the pursuit of honor in 13th century Iceland. Demonstrates that they constituted a unified semiotic system and suggests some comparative implications of these findings.

327. ———. "Settlement Patterns on the Frontiers of Folklore." In *Frontiers of Folklore*, edited by William R. Bascom, 121–31. AAAS Selected Symposium, 5. Boulder: Westview Press, [1977]. [o.p.]

The metaphoric title refers to author's description of the present state of current folklore theory. Describes the symposium (of which this paper was a part) as dealing with a basic reorientation in folklore from the concept of things to a mode of action, specifically communication. Outlines the beginning of "folklore as communication" with the ethnography of speaking, a subfield of linguistic anthropology termed by Dell Hymes in 1962. Also explores the matter of structural relationships surrounding the question, who are the folk? Concludes with the remark that the frontiers of folklore are largely bound up with anthropology and linguistics.

328. ———. *Story, Performance, and Event: Contextual Studies of Oral Narrative*. Cambridge Studies in Oral and Literate Culture, no. 10. Cambridge: Cambridge University Press, 1986.

A major work on performance practice in folklore, with special attention to the performance event itself. Corpus of 30 stories collected in Canton, Texas, on "First Monday" by the author over a 15 year period. Deals more with the act of storytelling than the text of the story. Demonstrates the interrelationships existing between events recounted in the stories, the texts, and the situations in which they are told. A close formal analysis of the texts is combined with an ethnographic examination of their telling, paying particular attention to the links between form and function.

329. ———. *Verbal Art as Performance*. 1977. Reprint. Prospect Heights, Ill.: Waveland Press, 1984.

Basic explanation and description of the study of performance events (ethnography of performance) including: 1) participant's identities and roles, 2) the expressive means employed in performance, 3) social interactional ground rules, norms, and strategies for performance and criteria for its interpretation and evaluation, and 4) the sequence of actions that make up the scenario of the event.

330. ——— and Joel Sherzer, eds. *Explorations in the Ethnography of Speaking*. Studies in the Social and Cultural Foundations of Language, no. 8. 1974. Reprint. New York: Cambridge University Press, 1989.

Collection of 21 essays follows in the tradition of Dell Hymes' work on the ethnography of speaking and is taken from the Austin conference on the same topic in 1972. Sections on communities and resources for performance, community ground rules for performance, speech acts, events and situations, shaping of artistic structures in performance and toward an ethnology of speaking. Good example of folklore research into performance; served as inspiration for ethnography of musical performance studies by Herndon and Brunyate (item 72); Herndon and McLeod (item 73); Stone (item 181) and Béhague (item 29).

331. Becker, Alton L. "Text-Building, Epistemology, and Aesthetics in Javanese Puppet Theatre." In *The Imagination of Reality: Essays in Southeast Asian Coherence Systems*, edited by A. L. Becker and Aram A. Yengoyan, 211–43. Norwood, N.J.: Ablex, 1979.

Dedicated to Geertz and interpretive/symbolic studies, the essay describes some of the constraints on text-building in Javanese shadow play, *wayang kulik*. Based on the author's lessons from a dalang, or puppeteer, 1967–71.

332. Becker, Howard. *Art Worlds*. Berkeley: University of California Press, 1982.

Recommended for its sociological insights into the analysis of music. Concerns itself more with the patterns of cooperation among the people who make the works of art than with the art work itself.

333. Bloch, Maurice. "Symbols, Song, Dance, and Features of Articulation: Is Religion an Extreme Form of Traditional Authority?" *Archives européenes de sociologie* 15/1 (1974):55–81.

Argues that symbols in ritual cannot be understood without a prior study of the nature of the communication medium of ritual in which they are embedded, in particular singing and dancing. Once this has been accomplished, symbols cannot anymore be understood as units of meaning in the Saussurian signifier/signified model.

334. Blu, Karen I. *The Lumbee Problem: the Making of an American Indian People*. Cambridge Studies in Cultural Systems; 5. Cambridge: Cambridge University Press, 1980.

Author traces the political and legal history of the Indians of Robeson County, arguing that their political activities have been powerfully affected by the interplay between their own and others' conceptions of who they are. The first documented study to employ both past and present circumstances in the analysis of what has happened to a nonreservation Eastern Indian people, of how they survived and managed to thrive despite strong efforts to discourage and disband them. Author uses Geertzian interpretive/symbolic method.

335. Boehmer, Konrad. "Sociology of Music." In *New Grove Dictionary of Music* 17 (1980):432–39.

Defines sociology of music as a discipline that examines the interrelationships of music and society. It is neither musicology nor sociology but may borrow from both whatever tools and techniques it requires to establish and implement the conceptual framework and methodology that is peculiar to itself. A helpful summary of the different approaches to research, e.g., positivism or Marxism. Compare definitions of the different terms that can often describe the same phenomenon but from a different perspective.

336. Bohannan, Paul J. and Mark Glazer, eds. *High Points in Anthropology*. New York: Alfred A. Knopf, 1973.

Book of readings resulting from editorial disagreement with Harris's *Rise of Anthropological Theory* (item 380) based on structural functionalism. Part III, Structure, Function, and Reciprocity, contains articles by Durkheim, Mauss, Malinowski, and Radcliffe-Brown.

337. Bourdieu, Pierre. *Distinction: A Social Critique of the Judgement of Taste*. Translated by Richard Nice. Cambridge, Mass.: Harvard University Press, 1984.

Originally published as *La Distinction: Critique sociale du jugement* (Paris: Les Editions de Minuit, 1979). Recommended for its sociological insights into the analysis of music. Proposes a model of the relationships between the universe of economic and social conditions and the universe of life-styles based on a rethinking of Max Weber.

338. ———. *Outline of a Theory of Practice*. Cambridge Studies in Social Anthropology, 16. Translated by Richard Nice. Cambridge: Cambridge University Press, 1977.

Originally published in French in 1972, this influential work seeks to define the prerequisites for a truly scientific discourse about human behavior, that is, an adequate theory of practice which must include a theory of scientific practice. Emphasis on process and performativity in contemporary anthropology.

339. Bowers, Jane and Judith Tick, eds. *Women Making Music: The Western Art Tradition, 1150–1950*. Urbana, Ill.: University of Illinois Press, 1986.

Contains 15 essays contributing to the study of music and gender. Purpose is to look at women's music—and women musicians themselves—by remembering them through the methods historians apply in their attempts to objectify the past.

340. Brenneis, Donald. "Performing Passions: Aesthetics and Politics in an Occasionally Egalitarian Community." *American Ethnologist* 14/2 (May 1987):236–50.

Advocating the study of emotion as part of performance theory, author examines nondiscursive features of a range of performance genres in a rural Fiji Indian village. The genres are found in verbal and musical performances alike.

341. Briggs, Jean L. *Never in Anger: Portrait of an Eskimo Family*. Cambridge, Mass.: Harvard University Press, 1970.

Representative of insider/outsider interaction, research is based on eight households of the Utkuhikhalingmuit people at the mouth of the Back River, northwest of Hudson Bay. Author is an anthropologist who became an "adopted daughter" of a family. Describes emotional patterning in the context of Utku life and draws a series of vignettes of individuals interacting with family and neighbors.

342. Bright, William. "Language and Music: Areas for Cooperation." *Ethnomusicology* 7/1 (Jan. 1963):26–32.

An early essay on language-and-music relationships by a linguist who participated in and was stimulated by Hood's U.C.L.A. seminars in ethnomusicology.

343. Brook, Barry S., Edward Downes and Sherman Van Solkema. *Perspectives in Musicology.* New York: Norton, 1972. Reprinted New York: Pendragon, 1985.

Collection of 15 lectures and transcripts of seminars delivered at City University of New York Graduate School, 1968–9. Inaugurated the doctoral program in musicology, and explored the state, methods, theories, and lacunae of present musicological research. Contains essays by Gilbert Chase, Nketia, Hood, Harrison. Reading list and select general bibliography included.

* SEE ALSO Chase, Gilbert. "American Musicology and the Social Sciences" (item 346).

344. Caraveli-Chaves, Anna. "Bridge between Worlds: The Greek Women's Lament as Communicative Event." *Journal of American Folklore* 93 (1980):129–57.

Author selected this Cretan village for her research because of the important function of poetry in all facets of daily life. Study focuses on the participants, what the lament convention does for them, and what they, through the convention, do for themselves. A contribution to performance theory.

345. ———. "The Symbolic Village: Community Born in Performance." *Journal of American Folklore* 98 (1985):259–86.

Demonstrates how, through performance, the guests of a *glendi* symbolically recreate the parameters of the actual village or urban community in which the most important relationships are enacted and new ones are negotiated. Fieldwork from Olymbos in Karpathos. Helpful for event analysis.

346. Chase, Gilbert. "American Musicology and the Social Sciences." In *Perspectives in Musicology,* edited by Barry S. Brook et al., 202–26. New York: Norton, 1972. Reprinted New York: Pendragon, 1985.

Explores the relationship of history to the social sciences, and with the relationship of both to musicology. Concludes that the term musicology should have the same sort of breadth, scope, and depth that the term anthropology has had in the social sciences.

Historical, systematic and comparative musicology should be major subdivisions without geographical, chronological, or cultural restrictions. Believes the term "comparative musicology" to mean the study of change, that "ethnomusicology" is too narrow, and proposes "cultural musicology" by analogy with "cultural anthropology."

347. Clifford, James. *The Predicament of Culture: Twentieth-Century Ethnography, Literature, and Art.* Cambridge: Harvard University Press, 1988.

A series of articles on critical ethnography of the West in its changing relations with other societies. Author is an historian with a strong interest in the human sciences, particularly cultural anthropology. Geertz has commented that Clifford is one of the few persons who connects history, literature, and anthropology. Provides a new perspective on the study of culture that might never have been generated from within anthropology itself [book jacket]. List of original article titles with later editions and major revisions indicated in "Sources," pp. 371–2. C. Waterman borrows Clifford's axiom that all human identities are from an historical point of view mixed, relational, and conjunctural (item 195).

348. Crapanzano, Vincent. *Tuhami: Portrait of a Moroccan.* 1980. Chicago: University of Chicago Press, 1986.

On the extremely complicated life history of a tilemaker married to a she-demon, a *jinniyya.* Also an attempt to make sense of what Tuhami told the author, in order to come to some understanding of how he articulated his world and situated himself within it. Shows concern about the anthropologist's responsibility to the people they study, and the recognition of ethical and political implications of the discipline. Represents the viewpoint of insider/outsider interaction.

349. Crawford, Richard. *American Studies and American Musicology: A Point of View and a Case in Point.* Institute for Studies in American Music Monograph no. 4. Brooklyn, New York: Institute for Studies in American Music, 1975.

Contains two essays, the first of which describes the increasing interest in American music studies just before the U.S. Bicentennial. He surveys the past in American music scholarship (particularly the monuments of literature), defines the traits of its studies, reflects on the differences between scholars of European and American music, and raises the question of the American historian/scholar as a participant in American musical life. A parallel case can be made for ethnomusicology.

350. Davis, Gerald L. *I Got the Word in Me and I Can Sing It, You Know; a Study of the Performed Afro-American Sermon.* Philadelphia: University of Pennsylvania Press, 1986.

Emic analysis based on three preachers' versions of "You're Just Not Ready" sermon, in the Bay Area. In Chapter 4 the author tests a model of the performed African-American sermon.

351. De Certeau, Michel. *The Practice of Everyday Life.* Translated by Steven Rendall. Berkeley: University of California Press, 1984. First published as: *L'invention du quotidien, I. Arts du faire.* Paris: UGE, 1980.

Develops the concepts of *strategies* as institution, place, and power based courses of action, whereas tactics are the non-institutionalized resources of the weak, depending on timing and not power. Outlines some important parameters and approaches for considering the practice-structure dialectic. In considering the value of "practice theory" as well as its more problematic aspects for musical ethnographers, Turino takes De Certeau and Bourdieu as a point of departure. Contains an enlightening "Preface to the English Translation," pp. ix-x, by the French author ("French experiences and expressions on its migration into the English language").

352. Devereux, George. *From Anxiety to Method in the Behavioral Sciences.* New Babylon Studies in the Behavioral Sciences, 3. The Hague: Mouton, 1967.

Takes as point of departure one of Freud's basic propositions, modified in the light of Einstein's conception of the source of scientific data, that it is counter-transference, rather than transference, which is the most critical datum of all behavioral sciences. From the viewpoint of insider/outsider interaction.

353. Diamond, Stanley, ed. *Toward a Marxist Anthropology: Problems and Perspectives.* World Anthropology series. The Hague: Mouton, 1979.

Papers resulting from a symposium on "Problems and Possibilities of a Marxist Ethnology" in 1973. The six sections— an existential opening, the structuralist constraint, primitive communism as theory and critique, African perspectives, ideological reflections, and some academic and bourgeois illusions—are combined with a semantic definition of Marxism, and a definition of structuralism.

354. Dolgin, Janet L. et al., eds. *Symbolic Anthropology: A Reader in the Study of Symbols and Meanings.* New York: Columbia University Press, 1977.

Includes 28 essays dealing with performance theory. "The invisible event" by Janet L. Dolgin and JoAnn Magdoff is perhaps the most enlightening. Looks at the relations between structure and event, history and myth, in our own culture. See also Barnett (item 324).

355. Dougherty, Janet W., ed. *Directions in Cognitive Anthropology.* Urbana: University of Illinois Press, 1985.

Designed to provide scholars and students with a collection of current research by cognitive anthropologists that reflects the contemporary breadth and underlying unity of the field. Strong emphasis upon current research.

356. Douglas, Mary. *Purity and Danger: An Analysis of Concepts of Pollution and Taboo.* New York: Frederick A. Praeger, 1966. Reprinted London, Boston: Ark Paperbacks, 1984.

The author, a British social anthropologist, tries to show that rituals of purity and impurity create unity in experience. States that in the 19th century there were two peculiarities which separated primitive religions as a block from the great religions of the world:

that the former were inspired by fear and confused with defilement and hygiene.

357. Duckles, Vincent. "Musicology." In *New Grove Dictionary of Music* 12 (1980): 836–63.

Adds a third view to the definition of musicology: the belief that the advanced study of music should be centered not on music but on man, the musician, acting within a social and cultural environment. Instructive to compare with definition of the sociology of music by Boehmer (item 335, especially pp. 836–46).

358. Dumont, Louis. *Homo Hierarchicus: The Caste System and its Implications.* Translated by Mark Sainsbury, Louis Dumont, and Basia Gulati. Rev. English ed. Chicago: University of Chicago Press, 1981, 1980.

Concerns the traditional social organization of India from the point of view of theoretical comparison. Representative of performance theory, with some influence from Lévi-Strauss and structuralism. Only English edition with the three appendices found in the French edition (1968).

359. Dundes, Alan. *The Study of Folklore.* Englewood Cliffs: Prentice-Hall, 1965.

Anthology of reprinted essays, many of them classics, by different authors and organized according to various aspects of the discipline: definition, origin, form, transmission, function, psychoanalysis, and selected studies. Each section begins with a short essay by Dundes and each paper is prefaced by a brief headnote.

360. Dwyer, Kevin. *Moroccan Dialogues: Anthropology in Question.* Baltimore: Johns Hopkins University Press, 1982. Reprinted Prospect Heights, Ill.: Waveland Press, 1987.

Finding himself at odds with traditional methods of field research, author used "event + dialogue" motif to examine his encounter with a person from another culture. In two parts, one a record of his fieldwork, and the second "On the Dialogic of

Anthropology" in which he reflects on his experience and questions the usual anthropological approaches. Representative of insider/outsider interaction.

361. Eames, Edwin and Judith Granich Goode. *Anthropology of the City; an Introduction to Urban Anthropology.* Prentice-Hall series in Anthropology. Englewood Cliffs, N.J.: Prentice-Hall, 1977.

Documents what was at that time termed "a new trend" or subfield of anthropology—"urban anthropology." Discusses the development of urban anthropology as related to the history of anthropology, in general the interface between urban anthropology and urban studies, especially in defining the nature of the "urban," and a concentration on those elements of the anthropological approach that adds to our understanding of urban life. Has proven useful for the study of urban ethnomusicology.

362. Fabian, Johannes. *Time and the Other: How Anthropology Makes Its Object.* New York: Columbia University Press, 1983.

A series of essays offered as studies of "anthropology through Time." Summary of anthropological history given in Chapter 5. Points particularly to Time in the act of producing ethnographic knowledge as well as the ideological nature of temporal concepts that influence ethnographer's theories and rhetoric, and intersubjective Time involved in fieldwork. Feels that scholars are on the threshold of some major change in conception of history and present role of anthropology. Mentioned by Blum (*EM* 34:418) as a profound study, which ethnomusicologists could do well to read and comment upon.

363. Falassi, Alessandro. *Folklore by the Fireside: Text and Context of the Tuscan "veglia."* Austin: University of Texas Press, 1980.

As an evening gathering of family and friends, the *veglia* includes regular performances of almost all genres of Tuscan folklore. Parallelism of narrative structure to the rites of passage are found in the texts. Tuscan worldview as manifested in different genres is consistent with respect to family values. Excellent example of performance theory in folklore.

364. Fogelson, Raymond. "The Cherokee Ballgame Cycle: An Ethnographer's View." *Ethnomusicology* 15/3 (September 1971): 327–338.

An interim report on a collaborative project with Herndon (item 70). Author's contribution involves ethnological and ethnographic data, both from secondary sources and from his own fieldwork. The general notion of transformation is used as a unifying theme to link social structural, cultural, and psychological levels of analysis. Provides a framework for further study and treatment.

365. Fox, Richard G. "Rationale and Romance in Urban Anthropology." *Urban Anthropology* 1/2 (1972): 205–33.

Makes a critical review of urban anthropology and proposes a redefinition of its purpose based on investigations of the ideological and behavioral links between cities and societies.

366. Friedman, Jonathan. "Marxism, Structuralism, and Vulgar Materialism." *Man* 9/3 n.s. (September 1974): 444–69.

Following up a 1971 AAA meeting, author summarizes a number of problems which he feels crucial to the future of anthropology: 1) critical areas of Marxism and structuralism, 2) structuralism of Lévi-Strauss (the ways in which structuralism might be incorporated into Marxism as well as indicating how certain ideological misinterpretations would oppose the two), 3) the new materialism of Sahlins, and 4) the cultural materialist causality of Harris.

367. Garfinkel, Harold. *Studies in Ethnomethodology.* Englewood Cliffs: Prentice-Hall, 1967. Reprinted London: Blackwell, 1985.

Collection of sociological essays that seek to treat practical activities, practical circumstances, and practical reasoning as topics of empirical study. By directing attention usually accorded extraordinary events to the most commonplace activities of daily life instead, the author seeks to learn about them as phenomena in their own right.

368. Geertz, Clifford. *The Interpretation of Cultures; Selected Essays.* New York: Basic Books, 1973.

A work which has influenced several ethnomusicologists working in interpretive/symbolic studies. Chapters 1, "Thick Description: Toward an Interpretive Theory of Culture" in which Geertz states his present position, and 15, "Deep Play: Notes on the Balinese Cockfight" are often cited. Geertz claims that all symbolic systems are historically constructed, socially maintained and individually applied.

369. ———. *Local Knowledge: Further Essays in Interpretive Anthropology.* New York: Basic Books, 1983, 1985.

A sequel to his *Interpretation of Cultures,* consisting of a collection of essays delivered to various audiences at different times. His humor and self-analysis make good reading.

370. Giddens, Anthony. *Central Problems in Social Theory: Action, Structure and Contradiction in Social Analysis.* Berkeley: University of California Press, 1979.

Continuation of a project which examines the residue of 19th century European social theory for contemporary problems of the social sciences. Intended as both a methodological and a substantive text. Chapters can be treated as self-contained entities, but "Agency, Structure; Institutions, Reproduction, Socialization" is particularly recommended. Representative of transactionalism in performance theory.

371. Glassie, Henry. *Passing the Time in Ballymenone; Culture and History of an Ulster Community.* Philadelphia: University of Pennsylvania Press, 1982.

A noted folklorist, Glassie presents a highly personal but well-documented record of Irish life. Amply illustrated with his own drawings and photographs. Includes description of a *ceili,* and the tunes for 19 songs. Over 100 pages of the total 852 contain Notes and Sources. Excellent example of performance theory as practiced in folklore.

372. ———, Edward D. Ives and John F. Szwed. *Folksongs and Their Makers*. Bowling Green: Bowling Green University Popular Press, [1969].

> Three essays on the process of creating a folksong by looking at the creator/performer and his social environment. Glassie writes on Dorrance Weir and "Take That Night Train to Selma," Ives on Joe Scott and "The Plain Golden Band," and Szwed on Paul E. Hall and "The Bachelor's Song." Each is a model for biography as a way to study the subjects of folksongs. Weir's song provides an opportunity to see how a folksong is made before it enters tradition. Because Scott printed and sold copies of his song, Ives was able to use written as well as aural evidence. Szwed's study is mostly concerned with what the songs meant to both singers and listeners.

373. Godelier, Maurice. *Perspectives in Marxist Anthropology*. R. Brain, translator. Cambridge Studies in Social Anthropology, 18. Cambridge: Cambridge University Press, 1977.

> Discussion of theoretical approaches which revolve continuously around anthropology and history to make them less incomprehensible and exasperating. Cautions never to accept anything as truth which has not first been questioned and proved correct.

374. Goldman, Irving. *Ancient Polynesian Society*. Chicago: University of Chicago Press, 1970; Ann Arbor: Books on Demand, UMI, n.d.

> Uses culture-area concept, as well as controlled comparison, as analytical methods. Studies the patterns of evolution of ancient Polynesian societies but began as an inquiry into sociology of elementary aristocracies. Useful for performance theory and studies.

375. Goody, Esther N., ed. *Questions and Politeness: Strategies in Social Interaction*. Cambridge Papers in Social Anthropology, 8. Cambridge: Cambridge University Press, 1978; Ann Arbor: Books on Demand, UMI, n.d.

> Essays are representative of transactionalism in performance theory. Sections include: towards a theory of questions, questions

of immediate concern, universals in language usage and the phenomena of politeness.

376. Gornick, Vivian, and Barbara K. Moran, eds. *Woman in Sexist Society: Studies in Power and Powerlessness*. New York: Basic Books, 1971. Reprint. New York: New American Library, 1972.

Collection of essays on gender and power. Demonstrates that woman's condition is the result of a slowly formed, deeply entrenched, pervasive cultural decision that woman shall remain a person defined not by the struggling development of her brain but rather by her childbearing properties and her status as companion to men, the movers and shakers who rule the earth.

377. Gregor, Thomas. *Mehinaku: The Drama of Daily Life in a Brazilian Indian Village*. Chicago: University of Chicago Press, 1977, 1980.

Uses symbolic interactionism to describe the way of life among one tribe of Mato Grosso Indians by viewing them as performers of social roles.

378. Hanna, Judith L. *The Performer-Audience Connection: Emotion to Metaphor in Dance and Society*. Austin: University of Texas Press, 1983.

On the communication of emotion in dance, expressly the history of attitudes that create expectations, what performers intend to convey and what spectators perceive. Some traces of past performances are thought to stay on in society through metaphors of dance. Good example of performance theory in practice.

379. Harris, Marvin. "The Cultural Ecology of India's Sacred Cattle." *Current Anthropology* 7/1 (Feb. 1966):51–66.

Attempts to indicate certain puzzling inconsistencies in prevailing interpretations of the ecological role of bovine cattle in India. Research is based on written sources, not fieldwork. Suggests that insufficient attention has been paid to such positive-functioned features of the Hindu cattle complex as traction power and milk, dung, beef and hide production in relationship to the costs of ecologically viable alternative. An interesting experiment.

380. ———. *The Rise of Anthropological Theory; a History of Theories of Culture.* New York: Crowell; London: Routledge and Kegan Paul, 1968. [o.p.]

At a time when anthropologists were being asked to help plan and carry out certain international development programs, author wanted to reassert the methodological priority of a search for the laws of history in the science of man. Feels strongly that anthropologists should take responsibility by understanding the basic principle of a macro-theory of socio-cultural evolution. As a result, the book can be read as a critical history of anthropological theories. Author hopes that the anthropologist can become more critical of research directions.

* Harrison, Frank Ll. "American Musicology and the European Tradition." SEE Harrison, Frank Ll. et al. *Musicology* (item 381).

381. ———, Mantle Hood and Claude V. Palisca. *Musicology.* Englewood Cliffs, N.J.: Prentice-Hall, 1963.

Commissioned by the Council of the Humanities of Princeton University to see what humanistic research has contributed to the culture of America and the world. Harrison's contribution, "American Musicology and the European Tradition," pp. 3–85, reviews the history of its subject with the suggestion that in the future it should involve a social approach as well as dare to look beyond the traditional boundaries for possibilities of study. Palisca's essay, "American Scholarship in Western Music," pp. 89–213, describes the special characteristics of its subject (in relationship to its relatively short history), its emergence and its achievements. Takes the position that the study of primitive and folk music belongs more in musicology than anthropology. The study of art music of non-Western cultures poses a more difficult problem. He concludes that inevitably there is one musicology and it includes the study of primitive, folk and art music. Hood's essay, "Music, the Unknown," pp. 217–326, concurs that the future of musicological inquiry lies in ethnomusicology, in areas yet to be explored. Representative of the time frame in which it was written, it describes the development and history of the discipline to date. Marks the beginning of a different mode of thinking about non-Western music: "through music, dance, and theater . . . can be revealed . . . all of those essential attributes making up the very identity of a people" (p. 326). See Merriam's review (*EM* 8/2:179–85) for an anthropological critique.

382. Hart, Keith. *The Political Economy of West African Agriculture.* Cambridge Studies in Social Anthropology, no. 43. Cambridge: Cambridge University Press, 1982.

Deals with the rise of commercial farming in West Africa. Specifically, what the various forms of agricultural commodity production have been and how the social life and economic structure of the region's communities have been affected by these developments. Believes it is analogous to the effect of the Industrial Revolution on Western Europe.

383. Hebdige, Dick. *Subculture: The Meaning of Style.* New Accents series. New York: Methuen, 1979.

Description of the process whereby objects are made to mean style in subculture. To decipher the meaning of style in subculture, the author adopts a number of approaches derived from semiotics and uses models drawn from European art and literature. An application of Marxist structuralism.

384. Heelas, Paul and Andrew Lock, eds. *Indigenous Psychologies: The Anthropology of the Self.* Language, Thought, and Culture series. London, New York: Academic Press, 1981.

Combines social psychology and anthropology in an application of performance theory, especially as it pertains to self and society. Described as the first systematic, interdisciplinary investigation of the nature of what people take themselves to be, or "indigenous psychology," according to the authors.

385. Herskovits, Melville J. "The Humanism in Anthropological Science." *Actes des VIe Congrès International des Sciences*

Anthropologiques et Ethnologiques, I:82–93. Paris: Musée de l'Homme, 1962.

An early plea for humanizing the essentially scientific orientation of anthropology. Stresses the need to recognize its importance in research and theory. Raises the question of whether we face a dichotomy that poses insurmountable problems in developing and utilizing concepts and methods deriving from a dual commitment. Hopes that the humanism in anthropology can be brought into balance and adequately integrated with its scientific orientation. Urges the consideration of the implications of this contradiction, to see whether some guide-posts towards its clarification can be constructed.

386. Herzfeld, Michael. "Performative Categories and Symbols of Passage in Rural Greece." *Journal of American Folklore* 94 (1981):44–57.

Attempts to elucidate certain features of Greek expressive culture. Specifically in the area of death and marriage, shows that two attempts to equate dirges with songs and a counter-proposal of an absolute taxonomic distinction between them oversimplify the situation. Concludes that the performative context determines what kind of passage is involved.

387. Holland, Dorothy and Naomi Quinn, eds. *Cultural Models in Language and Thought.* Cambridge: Cambridge University Press, 1987.

Following a cognitive anthropological approach, explores the way in which cultural knowledge is organized and used in everyday language and understanding. Employing a variety of methods which rely heavily on linguistic data, offers analyses of domains of knowledge ranging across the physical, social, and psychological worlds and reveal the crucial importance of tacit, presupposed knowledge in the conduct of everyday life.

388. Hutchinson, William. "Systematic Musicology Reconsidered." *Current Musicology* 21 (1976):61–9.

Reviews the principal sources on systematic musicology according to certain headings suggested by their common emphasis: 1) a comprehensive theoretical science of music, 2) selected interdisciplinary study of music, and 3) a correlative epistemological orientation within musicology. Identifies six problem-issues requiring continued discussion.

389. Hymes, Dell. "Folklore's Nature and Sun's Myth." *Journal of American Folklore* 88 (1975):345–69.

The author's presidential address to the American Folklore Society, 1974, concerning two issues: folklore and his rather critical conception of the discipline, and a myth text from the Kathlamet Chinook collected by Boas in 1890. The myth text is given, pp. 360–7, with a Synopsis, pp. 368–9.

390. ———. "Introduction: Towards Ethnographies of Communication." In *The Ethnography of Communication,* edited by John J. Gumperz and Dell Hymes, 1–34. Wisconsin: Special Publication—*American Anthropologist* 66/6:pt.2 (Dec. 1964). [o.p.]

Results of papers given in early 60s at anthropological meetings. Defines "ethnography of communication" and gives the components of communicative events as: the various kinds of participants, the various available channels, the codes shared by the participants, the settings in which communication takes place, the formal structure of the communication, the content of the communication, and the ethnographic status of the event. Has helped in defining performance theory studies in ethnomusicology.

391. ———. *Reinventing Anthropology.* New York: Pantheon Books, 1972.

A collection of essays grouped by sections titled: The Root is Man; Studying Dominated Cultures; Studying the Cultures of Power; Responsibilities of Ethnography; and The Root is Man: Critical Traditions. The introductory essay, "The Use of Anthropology: Critical, Political, Personal" (pp. 3–79), sets a critical but insightful mood that is also a positive one regarding present and future research and writing. Note the time frame in which it was written (end of 60s, early 70s). Blum refers to this title in reminding us we have a moral and professional obligation to be reinvented, that is, in relation to power and knowledge, and not to fall into the cultural despair of Foucault and Bourdieu (*EM* 34:420).

392. International Musicological Society. *Report of the 12th Congress, Berkeley, 1977.* Edited by Daniel Heartz and Bonnie C. Wade. Kassel: Bärenreiter, 1981.

Includes round table and discussion groups in 27 subject areas that occasionally mixes ethnomusicologists and musicologists. Porter's review (*EM* 29/3:524–7) remarks that the impact of ethnomusicology as it has developed since the 1950s, both in terms of its academic weight and the scope of its research methods, has never been so palpable, but that the real value of the report lies in the discussion sessions that follow formal papers.

393. Ives, Edward D. *Larry Gorman: The Man Who Made the Songs.* Indiana University Folklore series, no. 6. Bloomington: Indiana University Press, 1964.

This biography of a lumbercamp bard of the Northeast is a full study of a European-American folk creator. Gorman (1846–1917) was the author of numerous satirical songs which then went into the oral tradition. Ives hoped to shed some light on the creation of folksong and the relation of the individual songmaker to his tradition. Gorman is seen as part of the widespread traditional practice of making up satirical songs about people he knew. As satires they were a way of letting off steam. Those persons "songed" (i.e., satirized) usually accepted it and were even proud of it. Such songs were sung more for entertainment and lived on in the tradition as such. Excellent example of a biographical study of a musicians by a reputable folklorist.

394. Kahn, Joel S. *Minangkabau Social Formations: Indonesian Peasants and the World Economy.* Cambridge Studies in Social Anthropology, 30. Cambridge: Cambridge University Press, 1981.

On a form of peasant economic activity predominant in one part of West Sumatra during 1970 and 1972—the production and distribution of commodities on a small, often individual scale. Attempts to account for the predominance of this economic form in a specific place and time. A representative example of political economic theory in anthropology with potential application for ethnomusicology.

395. Kapferer, Bruce, ed. *Transaction and Meaning: Directions in the Anthropology of Exchange and Human Behavior*. A.S.A. Essays in Social Anthropology series, vol. 1. Philadelphia: Institute for the Study of Human Issues, 1979.

Essays derived from the 1973 Decennial Conference of the Association of Social Anthropologists of the Commonwealth entitled "New Directions in Social Anthropology." Especially recommended is McKim Marriott's "Hindu Transactions: Diversity Without Dualism," pp. 109–42, as representative of transactionalism in performance theory.

396. Kerman, Joseph. *Contemplating Music: Challenges to Musicology*. Cambridge, Mass.: Harvard University Press, 1985, 1986. English edition, Fontana Press/Collins, 1985, has title: *Musicology*.

A critical overview of musical research and activity in America and England after 1945, including music theory and composition, and ethnomusicology. A special chapter, "Ethnomusicology and 'Cultural Musicology,'" contains critical remarks on the field; includes Seeger and his framework for systematic musicology. Discusses the ethnomusicologist's critique of musicology and feels the former has done very little to help the latter. Assesses particularly the 1977 IMS congress and thinks only two panels— those on the oral transmission and concepts of mode—showed that ethnomusicological research is moving towards the study of Western music. Review by Porter is both critical and complimentary (in that order) and is directed to specific points rather than to Kerman's alleged misconceptions about ethnomusicology (*EM* 33/3:531–5). See also Blum's critical remarks and responses (item 41).

397. ———. "A Profile for American Musicology." *Journal of the American Musicological Society* 18/1 (Spring 1965):61–9.

Originally presented as a plenary session of A.M.S., 1964, Kerman praises *Musicology* by Harrison, Hood and Palisca (item 381) as a milestone in the history of the discipline. Quotes Palisca: "the musicologist is first and foremost an historian," and believes that Harrison pushes farther towards a "social aim," the understanding of man. Kerman suggests that critical insight could become another orientation of musicology because it does not exist on the American music scene. Criticizes in particular the lack of consideration for theory and analysis in *Musicology* and quotes Harrison's remarks on that subject: "musicology that has lost touch with music."

398. Kleinman, Arthur and Bryon Good, eds. *Culture and Depression: Studies in the Anthropology and Cross-Cultural Psychiatry of Affect and Disorder.* Comparative Studies of Health Systems and Medical Care series. Berkeley: University of California Press, 1985.

Believes strongly that a cross-cultural approach to research is important to advancing knowledge in these areas. Several essays written by anthropologists go far to unlock thinking about what depression is in non-Western culture. Representative of studies of self and society in relation to performance theory.

399. Kligman, Gail. "The Rites of Women: Oral Poetry, Ideology, and the Socialization of Peasant Women in Contemporary Romania." *Journal of American Folklore* 97 (1984):167–88.

Concentrates on certain aspects of the wedding rite, especially symbolic bargaining. Excellent example of performance theory as well as its treatment of gender issues.

400. Koskoff, Ellen, ed. *Women and Music in Cross-Cultural Perspective.* Contributions in Women's Studies, no. 79. New York: Greenwood Press, 1987. Reprint. Urbana, Ill.: University of Illinois Press, 1989.

In her introduction the editor surveys recent research in area of music and gender and frames discussion of various issues raised in light of contemporary anthropological insights. Topics are arranged geographically. Some are primarily musicological in orientation (Jones, Post, Coaldrake, Hassinger, Rothenbusch), others are genre studies based on historical and current practices (Cohen, Shehan, Sakata, Sutton, Petersen). The remainder are anthropological and contemporary descriptions and analyses of a variety of cultural/musical settings (Auerbach, see item 322; Koskoff, Roseman, Basso and Robertson). DjeDje reviews it as an excellent introduction to the on-going debate concerning women and music (*EM* 33/3:520). (See another collection of essays not included in the present bibliography: *Music, Gender, and Culture*, Marcia Herndon and Suzanne Ziegler eds. Wilhelmshaven: Florian Noetzel Verlag, 1990. Most of the articles were originally presented at a meeting of the Music and Gender Study Group of the ICTM in Heidelberg, Germany, 1988.)

401. Kuhn, Thomas S. *The Structure of Scientific Revolutions*. 2nd ed. International Encyclopedia of Unified Science. Foundations of the Unity of Science, vol. 2, no. 2. Chicago: University of Chicago Press, 1970.

A brief essay presents the author's fundamental objective: to urge a change in the perception and evaluation of familiar data. Identifies the source of the differences that lead him to recognize the role in scientific research of what he called "paradigms" (universally recognized scientific achievements that for a time provide model problems and solutions to a community of practitioners). A historically oriented view of science.

402. Langness, Lewis L. *The Study of Culture*. Chandler and Sharp Publications in Anthropology and Related Fields series. Rev. ed. Novato, Calif.: Chandler and Sharp, 1987.

Intended as a historically focused introduction to the study of cultural anthropology, or as the author proposes, for anyone who deals with the concept of culture. First published in 1974, it is work for the general student rather than the professional.

403. LaRue, Jan. *Guidelines for Style Analysis*. New York: Norton, 1970.

   Although intended for the analysis of Western music, the principles have sometimes provided a helpful basis for the analysis of non-Western music. Chapters devoted to fundamental analytical considerations, sound, harmony, melody, rhythm, the growth process, symbols for analysis and stereotypes of shape, evaluation and style.

404. Leach, Edmund. *Genesis as Myth and Other Essays*. Cape editions, 39. London: Jonathan Cape, 1969. [o.p.]

   A British social anthropologist of repute reprints three essays. The second two are titled "The Legitimacy of Solomon" and "Virgin Birth."

405. ———. *Rethinking Anthropology*. London School of Economics Monographs on Social Anthropology, no. 22. New York: Humanities Press; London: Athlone Press, 1966.

   A collection of seven essays dealing with themes not necessarily connected and representing a structuralist viewpoint that is still critical of certain aspects of British social anthropology.

406. Lee, Benjamin, ed. *Psychosocial Theories of the Self*. Path in Psychology series. New York: Plenum, 1982.

   Proceedings of an interdisciplinary conference on New Approaches to the Self (1979) in Chicago, which detailed developments in other disciplines. Anthropologists, psychoanalysts and developmental psychologists made up the group of participants. At that moment it represented a groundswell of activity in the investigation of the self because there was the discovery of the importance of problems of meaning and interpretation in psychology and anthropology.

407. Levy, Robert I. *Tahitians: Mind and Experience in the Society Islands*. Chicago: University of Chicago Press, 1973. Reprint. Chicago: University of Chicago, Midway, 1988.

A study as much about the author as about his informants, and thus a study of self and society as well as performance. Book is directed toward two audiences, not necessarily relevant to one another: 1) those interested in the natural history of this sample of Polynesian life, and 2) those concerned with problems of psychological anthropology and personality theory.

408. Limón, José E. "History, Chicano Joking, and the Varieties of Higher Education: Tradition and Performance as Critical Symbolic Action." *Journal of the Folklore Institute* 19 (May-Dec. 1982): 141–66.

Argues for an alternative interpretation of the joking traditions, which emphasizes their socially critical, rather than their integrative, psychological significance. Focus on Paredes' "Stupid American" joke cycle. Contextual meaning reveals the influence of performance as an approach to folklore. Full analysis of folkloric action and its symbolic meanings requires a substantial delineation of its social context in both synchronic and diachronic modes.

409. ———. "Legendry, Metafolklore and Performance: A Mexican-American Example." *Western Folklore* 42 (1983): 191–207.

Application of performance theory to a Mexican-American variant of the Vanishing Hitchhiker legend. Stresses the human actors in a verbal art. Term "metafolklore" comes from Dundes' concept "to refer to folkloristic statements about folklore." Questions the concept of belief as the linking fundamental element in the particular metafolkloric relationship of legend and anti-legend. Sees Mexican-American artistic competence displayed as symbolic action that speaks ideologically to issues of gender and ethnicity.

410. ———. "Western Marxism and Folklore: A Critical Introduction." *Journal of American Folklore* 96 (Jan.-Mar. 1983): 34–52.

On the place of folklore in the development of so-called non-Soviet Marxism, specifically among selected and representative nonfolklorists who the author calls Western Marxists. Contends, however, that their treatment of folklore has a limited character.

Concludes with a tentative outline for a more adequate Marxist folkloristics.

411. ———. "Western Marxism and Folklore: A Critical Reintroduction." *Journal of American Folklore* 97 (July-Sept. 1984): 337–44.

Reacts to Zipes's comments on his [Limón's] earlier essay (item 468). Expands and demonstrates that it adequately achieves what he meant it to do.

412. ——— and M.J. Young. "Frontiers, Settlements, and Development in Folklore Studies, 1972–1985." *Annual Review of Anthropology* 15 (1986): 437–60.

Critical review of a particular direction being taken in the contemporary anthropological study of folklore. Discusses a new conceptual approach to the study of folklore which emerged in the early and mid-1970s—performance and contextually centered understandings of folklore as social behavioral process and as situated communicative interaction. Includes remarks about Porter's 1976 Jeannie Robertson article (item 134).

413. Lindsay, Peter and Donald A. Norman. *Human Information Processing: an Introduction to Psychology.* 2nd ed. New York: Academic Press, c1977.

The second edition of the book is "desexed" and written to reflect recent developments as well as anticipate new directions.

414. Lowinsky, Edward. "Character and Purposes of American Musicology: a Reply to Joseph Kerman." *Journal of the American Musicological Society* 18/2 (Summer 1965): 222–34.

Challenges Kerman's contention (see item 397) that criticism should be musicology's true aim and feels he failed to back up his statement. Most branches of musicological science stand on the degree to which they follow the principles of their disciplines. They are original to the extent to which they evolve new procedures, discover new sources, and apply new criteria emerging from the problems inherent in the disciplines themselves. Feels that criticism doesn't influence any of these.

415. Lutz, Catherine and Geoffrey M. White. "The Anthropology of Emotions." *Annual Review of Anthropology* 15 (1986): 405–36.

Examines the last decade of American anthropological research on emotions. Begins by looking at some of the theoretical and epistemological tensions which serve to structure both debates and silences on the relationship between emotion and culture.

416. Marcus, George E. and Michael M.J. Fischer. *Anthropology as Cultural Critique: an Experimental Moment in the Human Sciences.* Chicago: University of Chicago Press, 1986.

An effort to clarify the present situation of cultural and social anthropology (not intended as a history nor as a complete bibliographic survey). Focuses on American developments with applications to British which strongly influenced the American during the 60s. Remarks that today the position has reversed and the American guides the British. The third major tradition, the French, is now influencing the American. Forges a useful discourse about contemporary and future work. In writing about musical practice and representation, C. Waterman (*EM* 34:367) quotes the authors as stating, "what makes representation so challenging is the perception that the 'outside forces' in fact are an integral part of the construction and constitution of the 'inside,' the cultural unit itself, and must be so registered, even at the most intimate levels of cultural process" (p. 77).

417. Marsella, Anthony J., George DeVos and Francis L.K. Hsu, eds. *Culture and Self: Asian and Western Perspectives.* London, New York: Tavistock, 1985.

A comprehensive resource for understanding the reciprocal relationships between culture and self in Western and Asian thought, as well as the implications for human adaptation and adjustment. A cross-cultural exploration of "self." Discussion of both historical and contemporary concepts in scholarly literature.

418. Meeker, Michael E. *Literature and Violence in North Arabia.* Cambridge Studies in Cultural Systems, 3. Cambridge: Cambridge University Press, 1979.

Re-examines the relationship of human character and natural conditions among the pastoralists (nomadic herders). Draws on the work of Western ethnographers who observed Bedouins around the turn of the century. Author studied with Geertz and follows his interpretive/symbolic studies.

419. Meyer, Leonard B. *Music, the Arts and Ideas: Patterns and Predictions in Twentieth Century Culture.* Chicago: University of Chicago Press, 1967. Paperback, 1969.

In attempting to understand the present, and to discover some pattern and rationale in the perplexing world of 20th century culture, centers on music but includes the ideas and beliefs of other arts. Explores the hypothesis that a number of alternative styles of music will be developed in contemporary times in a kind of dynamic steady-state. Last section concerns the perceptual-cognitive problems posed by highly complex music. Reviewed by Hutchinson (*EM* 13:378–9) and Chase (*Notes* 25/2:225–7).

420. Moore, Kenneth. "The City as Context: Context as Process." *Urban Anthropology* 4/1 (1975):17–25.

Views urban context as a process of change and suggests that the core of urban culture is to be found in the ways diversity is integrated in processes of creative change. Influenced urban ethnomusicology.

421. Moore, Sally Falk and Barbara G. Myerhoff. *Symbol and Politics in Communal Ideology: Cases and Questions.* Symbol, Myth and Ritual series. Ithaca: Cornell University Press, 1975.

Deals with the pursuit of communal harmony in planned, nonplanned, and antiplanned communities. Fruitfully applies the extended-case method in linking particular cases and situations to larger social context and to larger theoretical problems. Five essays by different authors plus an Epilogue in two parts: 1) the idealization of spontaneity and 2) the idealization of tradition and regulation. Represents the school of symbolic anthropology closely associated with the work of Victor Turner.

422. Munn, Nancy D. "The Effectiveness of Symbols in Murngin Rite and Myth." In *Forms of Symbolic Action; American Ethnology Society Proceedings*, 1969, edited by Robert F. Spencer, 178–207. Seattle: University of Washington Press, 1969. Reprint. New York, AMS Press, 1988.

Examines the nexus between an important Murngin myth and its associated rituals. As a follower of Turner's symbolic anthropology, author expresses concern with collective symbolic forms as instruments for transforming subjective experience. Specific thesis is that the myth conveys body destruction images saturated with negative feeling which the rituals convert into feelings of well-being.

423. Myerhoff, Barbara G. *Peyote Hunt: The Sacred Journey of the Huichol Indians*. Symbol, Myth and Ritual series. Ithaca: Cornell University Press, 1976.

Insightful study of Huichol Indians and the richly complex meaning of Mexican religion and world view. Author worked closely with a shaman-priest and participated in a sacred pilgrimage. As a follower of Turnerian symbolic anthropology, the author relates the shaman's own story and interpretation of his culture's customs and symbols.

424. Narmour, Eugene. *Beyond Schenkerism: the Need for Alternatives in Music Analysis*. Chicago: University of Chicago Press, 1977. Paperback, 1980.

Attempts to refute principal beliefs of Schenkerian theory and to dispute many of the analytical practices of its followers. His first concern is to demonstrate that Schenkerian voice-leading principles produce analytical results that are indefensible. Second, explores the conceptual basis of an implication-realization model. Third major area of discussion is on matters of style theory and analytical criticism. Also discusses the relationship of the theorist to history.

425. O'Laughlin, Bridget. "Mediation of a Contradiction: Why Mbum Women Do Not Eat Chicken." In *Woman, Culture and Society*, ed. by Michelle Zimbalist Rosaldo and Louise Lamphere, 301–18. Stanford: Stanford University Press, 1974.

Description of the basis of sexual asymmetry in a village in Southwestern Tchad. Dominance of men is based primarily on their control of the forces and means of reproduction (women and surplus), rather than on any technologically defined or natural division of labor. Marxian theory is discussed at length.

426. Ortner, Sherry B. "Gods' Bodies, Gods' Food: A Symbolic Analysis of a Sherpa Ritual." In *The Interpretation of Symbolism*, ed. by Roy Willis,133–69. A.S.A. Studies, 3. New York: Wiley; London: Malaby Press, 1975. [o.p.]

In using Geertz's system of symbols idea, author performs a symbolic analysis of Sherpa ritual. Issues raised go beyond the paper's immediate scope: 1) the enormously complex Sherpa ritual and religious system, 2) the relationship between a "high" religion and its popular practice, and 3) ritual and the processes of symbolic action, particularly the constant intertransposition of form and content. Virtually every element of the ritual can be seen to function as both part of its problematic (its "content") and part of its modes of solution (its "form").

427. ———. "Theory in Anthropology Since the Sixties." *Comparative Studies in Society and History* 26 (1984):126–66.

Scrutinizes the present more closely and finding it rather disorderly, author argues it is possible to discern the shape of the order to come. Sees a new key symbol of theoretical orientation is emerging, which may be labeled "practice" (or "action" or "praxis"). It is neither a theory nor a method in itself, but a symbol, in the name of which a variety of theories and methods are being developed. A good review of the relations between various theoretical schools or approaches in anthropology.

428. Osgood, Charles E., William H. May and Murray S. Miron. *Cross-Cultural Universals of Affective Meanings*. Urbana: University of Illinois Press, 1975.

Represents an early step in Osgood's concern with the measurement of meaning. Very specific and detailed; a potential goldmine of quantitative information about universals, subuniversals, and uniqueness in human semantic systems and subjective cultures more generally. Project was designed to test the hypothesis that regardless of language or culture, human beings use the same qualifying (descriptive) framework in allocating the affective meanings of concepts.

* Palisca, Claude V. "American Scholarship in Western Music." SEE Harrison, Frank Ll. et al. *Musicology* (item 381).

429. Peña, Manuel H. *The Texas-Mexican Conjunto: History of a Working-Class Music*. Mexican American Monographs, 9. Austin: University of Texas Press, 1985.

Interpretive history of a highly popular type of accordion music. Attempts to link the musical culture theoretically to its social base. Reflects influence of Marxism as well as insider/outsider research technique.

430. Pike, Kenneth L. *Language in Relation to a Unified Theory of the Structure of Human Behavior*. Janua linguarum. Series maior; 24. The Hague: Mouton, 1967, 1971.

Important for its explanation of the use of *etic* and *emic* in the description of behavior. Etic studies view behavior from outside a particular system, and emic from the inside. Other characteristics are: etic treats all cultures at the same time, emic one culture at a time; etic units and classification may be available before one begins analysis, emic is determined during analysis; etic organization of a worldwide cross-cultural scheme may be created by the analyst, emic must be discovered; etic does not require every unit to be viewed as part of a larger setting, emic does; etic data are obtainable early in analysis with partial information, emic requires a knowledge of the total system; and etic data provide access into the system (a starting point giving tentative results), emic units give final analysis or presentation.

431. Popper, Karl R. *Conjectures and Refutations.* 4th ed. London: Routledge and Kegan Paul, 1972.

In developing a theory of knowledge, growth evolves by conjectures (unjustified anticipations, guesses, and tentative solutions to our problems). These in turn are controlled by criticism, or attempted refutations. In other words, we learn from our mistakes.

432. Rabinow, Paul. *Reflections on Fieldwork in Morocco.* Quantum books. Berkeley: University of California Press, 1977.

Reflecting insider/outsider research in anthropology, notes that the collection of cultural data shapes and informs the collected material and its participant observer. Centers on the mutual construction of activities and communication by the anthropologist and the people he works with in the field.

433. Rappaport, Roy A. *Pigs for the Ancestors: Ritual in the Ecology of a New Guinea People.* 2nd ed. New Haven: Yale University Press, 1984.

On the Tsembaga living in the Bismarck Mountains. Concerns how ritual affects relationships between a congregation and entities external to it, rather than the part ritual plays in relationships within a congregation. This aspect of human ecology has been little explored. The revised edition addresses discussion provoked by the original book.

434. Reiter, Rayna R., ed. *Toward an Anthropology of Women.* New York: Monthly Review Press, 1975.

Collection of 17 articles with roots in the women's movement that provides some guidelines and examples of directions for an anthropology of women. Resulted from an attempt to organize and teach a course on women from an anthropological perspective. Cautions against the potential for male bias in anthropological accounts, both the bias brought to research by the researcher and the bias received if the society studied expresses male dominance. Cites the need for more studies that will focus on women but with a redefinition and re-examination of questions and theories.

435. Riesman, Paul. Freedom in Fulani Social Life: An Introspective Ethnography. Translated by Martha Fuller. Chicago: University of Chicago Press, 1977.

   Details fieldwork among the Jelgobe of Upper Volta. Investigates concepts of freedom in the language and behavior of the Fulani themselves. Reflecting insider/outsider interaction, the second part of the book is an introspective ethnography in which the author describes his experiences among the Fulani.

436. Rosaldo, Michelle Zimbalist. *Knowledge and Passion: Ilongot Notions of Self and Social Life*. Cambridge Studies in Cultural Systems, 4. Cambridge: Cambridge University Press, 1980.

   Documents enduring and intelligible Ilongot social action and, by exploring views of their emotional life as it relates to conduct in their social world, relates some consistent themes in their activity and thought. Method incorporates Geertzian interpretive/symbolic studies, as well as insider/outsider interaction.

437. ———— and Louise Lamphere, eds. *Women, Culture and Society*. Stanford: Stanford University Press, 1974.

   Papers represent a first generation's attempt to integrate an interest in women into a general theory of society and culture. Outlines a number of theoretical issues, and illustrates lines of thought that later studies might pursue. Includes Bridget O'Laughlin's "Mediation of a Contradiction: Why Mbum Women Do Not Eat Chicken" (item 425) and Bette S. Denich's "Sex and Power in the Balkans."

438. Rosen, Charles. *The Classical Style: Haydn, Mozart, Beethoven*. Rev. ed. London: Faber and Faber, 1976. First published: New York: Norton Library, 1971.

   Significant for its discussion of musical style, theories of form and coherence of musical language. Believes that the true inheritors of classical style were not those who maintained its traditions but those who preserved its freedom and at the same time altered and ultimately destroyed its musical language.

439. Rosen, Lawrence. "The Negotiation of Reality: Male-Female Relations in Sefrou, Morocco." In *Women in the Muslim World*, edited by Lois Beck and Nikke Keddie, 561–84. Cambridge: Harvard University Press, 1978.

Example of a conversation between an older Moroccan man and the wife of a friend regarding the coming arranged marriage of the woman's daughter. Analyzed in a Geertzian interpretive/symbolic light. The participants negotiated through and about their views of what was really true about their common situation in order to be able to comprehend its nature and take some meaningful action.

440. Sahlins, Marshall D. "Culture and Environment: The Study of Cultural Ecology." In *Horizons of Anthropology*, edited by Sol Tax and Leslie G. Freeman, 132–47. 2nd ed. Chicago: Aldine, 1977. [o.p.]

Written in the hope that if anthropology and its sister human sciences keep pace with the accumulating consequences of dominance, then the development of the ecological perspective will have first requisite.

441. ———. *Historical Metaphors and Mythical Realities: Structure in the Early History of the Sandwich Islands Kingdom.* Association for Social Anthropology in Oceania,. A.S.A.O. Special Publication, 1. Ann Arbor: University of Michigan Press, 1981.

Emphasizes process and performativity in contemporary anthropology. Argues that a confrontation of cultures affords a privileged occasion for seeing very common types of historical change. Book is part of a larger, wider study project.

442. ———. *Islands of History.* Chicago: University of Chicago Press, 1985.

Holds the thesis that historical events can become meaningful only when they are placed in a pre-existing cultural order, but a culture's way of understanding the world can be changed in and by unexpected events. Maintains that anthropological thinking needs to shift away from its current focus on the ethnographic present and to examine instead patterns and interpretations of events from which structures of meaning grow.

443. ———. *Stone Age Economics*. Chicago: Aldine de Gruyter, 1974, c1972. London: Tavistock, 1974.

Perpetuates the possibility of an anthropological economics by giving a few concrete examples. Written from the point of view of Marxist structuralism.

444. ——— and Elman R. Service, eds. *Evolution and Culture*. Ann Arbor: University of Michigan Press, 1982. [o.p.]

At the time of the original publication (1960) these essays constituted the best treatment of cultural evolutionism. The authors—Thomas G. Harding, David Kaplan, Marshall D. Sahlins and Elman R. Service—were all young scholars who accepted cultural evolutionism from the beginning.

445. Sarana, Gopala. *The Methodology of Anthropological Comparisons: an Analysis of Comparative Methods in Social and Cultural Anthropology*. Viking Fund Publications in Anthropology, no. 53. Tucson: University of Arizona Press, 1975.

Purpose is to make an analytical study of different comparative methods. Deals with the subject-matter, purpose, and techniques or procedures used by the anthropologist in his comparisons. Concepts and conceptualization, as well as the traditional problem of inductive and deductive reasoning and their respective places in science, are also discussed. Concludes that comparative procedures do not offer an explanation, but rather are a means for concept formation and clarification.

446. Schieffelin, Edward L. "Performance and the Cultural Construction of Reality." *American Ethnologist* 12/4 (Nov. 1985): 707–24.

Examines the limitations of a meaning-centered approach by showing that in Kaluli curing seances, the force of the transformation comes across on the nondiscursive dramaturgical and rhetorical levels of performance. Illustrative of performance theory. Steven Feld worked with the author and his wife, Bambi.

447. ———. *The Sorrow of the Lonely and the Burning of the Dancers.* New York: St. Martin's, 1976. Reprint. St. Lucia [Australia]: University of Queensland Press, 1977.

Influenced by Lévi-Strauss and Bateson, the author writes about Kaluli ceremonies and reciprocity, community, food, organization, the unseen, assertion and appeal, emotions, and specific ceremonies, particularly the *gisaro* ("pulling out the grubs"). Compares the Journey of the Dead, the curing process, and *gisaro* within the framework of opposition scenario, that is, the Kaluli's perception of their world in relations of opposition. The problem of comprehending many kinds of events resolves itself into understanding the nature of the opposition that gives form to them.

448. Schneider, Jane and Peter Schneider. *Culture and Political Economy in Western Sicily.* Studies in Social Discontinuity series. New York: Academic Press, 1976.

Treats factors such as the early export of wheat and animal products, and on the loss of manpower through emigration, as well as the rise and development of the Mafia. In addition, analyzes cultural codes that recognize honor, cleverness, and friendship and that are salient to contemporary social organization. Like emigration and the Mafia, culture is held to be the product of determinant historical processes—processes of dominance, subordination, and local reactions to dominance in relations between Sicily and more powerful populations centuries earlier.

449. Shepherd, John, Phil Virden, Graham Vulliamy, and Trevor Wishart. *Whose Music? A Sociology of Musical Languages.* New Brunswick, N.J.: Transaction Books; London: Latimer, 1977.

The central theme, that music is an aspect of a wider social reality, is approached from diverse perspectives—musical, aesthetic, sociological, and education. Breaks new ground and stimulates a re-examination of traditional assumptions about music, and in the process opens up new avenues for both research and activity. Incorporates a Marxist approach in the sociology of music.

450. Shweder, Richard A. and Robert A. LeVine, eds. *Culture Theory: Essays on Mind, Self and Emotion.* Cambridge: Cambridge University Press, 1984.

Collection of essays, the product of a Social Science Research Council conference in New York City, representing a stage in the development of the so-called symbols-and-meanings conception of culture. Looks at conceptual and methodological problems in the definition and study of meaning, and shows how the study of meaning can help answer questions about the origins of mind, self and emotion. Michelle Rosaldo's contribution, "Toward an Anthropology of Self and Feeling," a synthesis of her previous thinking about the creative power and symbols, was the last before her accidental death during field research.

451. Southall, Aidan, ed. *Urban Anthropology: Cross-Cultural Studies of Urbanization.* New York: Oxford University Press, 1973.

Papers resulting from a seminar held at Burg Wartenstein, Austria, Sept. 1964, sponsored by the Wenner-Gren Foundation for Anthropological Research. At the time of the seminar there was a new emphasis on urban anthropology, especially the teaching of it. Includes studies on Africa, Latin America, Japan, India, Indonesia and the Pacific. Has influenced urban ethnomusicology.

452. Sparshoot, Frederick E. "Aesthetics of Music." In *The New Grove Dictionary of Music and Musicians* 1 (1980):120–34.

Contains brief sections on definition (the philosophy of the meaning and value of music), kinds of writing, major periods of philosophical thought, musical subdivisions, and aesthetics in other civilizations. Accompanying bibliography follows same divisions.

453. Sudnow, David. *Ways of the Hand: The Organization of Improvised Conduct.* Cambridge: Harvard University Press, 1978. Reprint. New York: Harper Colophon Books, 1981.

Author's background as a jazz pianist plays a large part in his choice of the human hand to clarify the nature of the human body and its creations. Concerns description more than explanation.

Discusses the question of whether the body's improvisational ways can be closely described from the viewpoint of the performer, not through an introspective consciousness, but by a fine examination of concrete problems posed by the task of sustaining an orderly activity.

454. Tambiah, Stanley J. "The Magical Power of Words." *Man* 3/2, n.s. (June 1968):175–208.

The ingredients of most ritual systems in which there is a reciprocal relation between the word and the deed are: the word, the thought, the notion of power, and the deed. Makes the point that ritual words cannot be treated as an undifferentiated category. Uses a single class of rituals practiced in Ceylon as an example.

455. Terray, Emmanuel. *Marxism and "Primitive" Societies: Two Studies*. Translated by Mary Klopper. Modern Reader, PB-214. New York: Monthly Review Press, 1972. [o.p.]

Two studies prepared independently but both concerned with the study of "primitive societies" and the relevance of historical materialism (the science of social development). "Morgan and Contemporary Anthropology" is a critical examination of traditional ethnological theory starting from a historically decisive point. "Historical Materialism and Segmentary and Lineage-Based Societies" shows the signs of a changing climate by analyzing Claude Meillassoux's *Anthropologie économique des Gouro de Côte d'Ivoire* (The Hague: Mouton, 1964).

456. Tunstall, Patricia. "Structuralism and Musicology: An Overview." *Current Musicology* 27 (1979):51–64.

Summary description of Saussure and Lévi-Strauss in the application and development of structuralist theory and practice. Author responds to the question: what is the relation of structuralism to musicology? Although there have been a variety of methods and goals that are difficult to classify and summarize, they all began by applying structural linguistic methods to musicological endeavors. Discussed at length are musical semiotics and application of Lévi-Strauss' general anthropological orientation and particularly his hypothesis that music is an appropriate object for structuralist attention.

457. Turner, Victor W. *Dramas, Fields and Metaphors: Symbolic Action in Human Society.* Symbol, Myth and Ritual Series. Ithaca: Cornell University Press, 1974. Reprint. 1975.

Contains seven essays, four of which were previously published. Attempts to probe and describe the ways in which social actions of various kinds acquire form through metaphors and paradigms in their performers' minds and sometimes generate new forms, metaphors and paradigms.

458. ———. *The Forest of Symbols; Aspects of Ndembu Ritual.* Ithaca: Cornell University Press, 1967. Reprint. 1986.

An often quoted collection of previously published essays arranged in chronological order. Introduction summarizes the salient features of village and vicinage structure as well as outlines the ritual system. Falls into two sections: 1) mainly theoretical treatments of symbolism and witchcraft, and 2) descriptive accounts of aspects of ritual. Observes that it was an enriching experience to note the contrast between the relatively simple and monotonous economic and domestic life of Ndembu hunters and hoe cultivators, and the ordered arrangement and colorful symbolism of their religious life.

459. ———. "Frame, Flow and Reflection: Ritual and Drama as Public Liminality." In *Performance in Post-Modern Culture*, edited by Michael Benamou and Charles Caramello, 33–55. Milwaukee: Center for Twentieth Century Studies, University of Wisconsin-Milwaukee, 1977. (Theories of Contemporary Culture, 1).

Discusses the author's ideas about relationships between drama and reflection, performance and public reflexivity, talking or "doing" codes and drama, public reflexivity and liminality (he likens liminal in the socio-cultural process to the subjunctive mood in verbs), and liminality and experiment/play (play of ideas, words, symbols, metaphors). Uses Van Gennep's definition of liminality to mean the second of three stages in a "rite of passage," or that stage of "margin or limen" (threshold) when the subjects of ritual fall into a limbo between their past and present modes of daily existence. Distinguishes between everyday social space and liminal space. Follows psychologist Csikszentmihalyi's six attributes of flow in drama, and in relating flow's relationship to frame and reflexivity, the frame analysis of Erving Goffman. Distinguishes between liminal and liminoid genres.

460. ———. *From Ritual to Theatre: the Human Seriousness of Play.* Performance Studies series, 1. New York: Performing Arts Journal Publications, 1982.

Includes four essays that chart the author's personal discovery from traditional anthropological studies of ritual performance to a lively interest in modern theater, particularly experimental theater. Turner's perspective was adapted into play studies in folklore, as was his development of "an anthropology of performance," which likewise influenced folklore performance studies.

461. ———. "Liminal to Liminoid, in Play, Flow and Ritual: an Essay in Comparative Symbology." In *The Anthropological Study of Human Play,* edited by Edward Norbeck, 53–92. Rice University Studies, vol. 60, no. 3. Houston: Rice University, 1974.

After defining comparative symbology and how it differs from disciplines like semiotics and symbolic anthropology, the author discusses some sociocultural processes and settings in which new symbols are generated. Looking at symbols in movement, observes that they can be played against possibilities of form and meaning. Discusses liminal and liminoid (products) situations as settings where new symbols, models and paradigms arise.

462. ———. *The Ritual Process; Structure and Anti-Structure.* The Lewis Henry Morgan Lectures, 1966. Chicago: Aldine; London: Routledge and Kegan Paul, 1969. Reprint with Foreword. Symbol, Myth and Ritual series. Ithaca: Cornell University Press, 1977.

Falls into two main sections: 1) the symbolic structure of Ndembu ritual and the semantics of that structure, and 2) the social rather than symbolic properties of the liminal phase of ritual. Particular attention paid to "communitas" or an "extra"-structural or "meta"-structural modality of social interrelationship. Helpful in event analysis.

463. Tyler, Stephen A., ed. *Cognitive Anthropology; Readings.* New York: Holt, Rinehart and Winston, 1969. Reprint. Prospect Heights, Ill.: Waveland Press, 1987.

An anthology with two goals: 1) to provide a basic text in cognitive anthropology for undergraduate and graduate students, and 2) to bring together a collection of essays, for anthropologists and scientists in related disciplines, that are representative of assumptions, methods, problems, and results in cognitive anthropology. Believes that the aims and procedure of cognitive anthropology have profound implications not only for anthropology, but allied disciplines as well.

464. Voget, Fred W. *A History of Ethnology.* New York: Holt, Rinehart and Winston, 1975. [o.p.]

Traces the intellectual history of cultural anthropology with special emphasis on ethnology. Approaches anthropology from four perspectives: 1) as an institutional development of Western civilization, 2) as cumulative and as the result of historical and evolutionary processes normally affecting any institution, 3) as having a destiny linked to a special subject matter ("reality" problem), and 4) as confronting broad metaphysical and epistemological issues that must be accommodated if advances in controlled observation, analysis, and generalization are to be achieved.

465. Ward, John M. "The Hunt's Up." *Proceedings of the Royal Musical Association* 106 (1980):1–25.

Purpose is to establish the relationships between the various aspects of the musical entity, "The Hunt's Up": as a ground, a type of song, a few pieces of instrumental music, a musical genre, and a custom. Concludes that although the evidence is in writing, the music was orally transmitted in the Renaissance as well as the 20th century. Considering that orally transmitted music is a process and that a tune has a collection of possibilities, looks for common features of the different versions. Tune has stayed multiform and stable since the time of John Gay and has retained the characteristics of a discant to the "Hunt's Up" ground. Valuable for author's research process, work-up of available information, and witty writing style.

466. Whitten, Norman. "Ritual Enactment of Sex Roles in the Pacific Lowlands of Ecuador-Colombia." *Ethnology* 13/2 (April 1974):129–43.

Deliberate attempt to merge the analysis of exotic and prosaic, distinctive and non-distinctive ritual with a discussion of social structure. Analysis of the secular *currulao* or marimba dance plays a central part.

467. Yalman, Nur. "The Structure of Sinhalese Healing Rituals." In *Religion in South Asia*, ed. by Edward B. Harper, 115–50. Seattle: University of Washington Press, 1964. [o.p.]

Deals with ritual rather than myth, but has been influenced by Lévi-Strauss's analysis of myth. Thesis is that rituals (as myths) are also centered around basic contradictions such as pollution and purity, fortune and misfortune, health and illness, etc., and appear to try to turn the one into the other. From the Conference on Religion in South Asia, 1961, University of California, Berkeley.

468. Zipes, Jack. "Folklore Research and Western Marxism: A Critical Replay." *Journal of American Folklore* 97 (July-Sept. 1984):329–37.

Reacts to José Limón's article of the previous year (item 411), particularly regarding the point that the contribution of Western Marxists to folklore research is limited. Clarifies the author's position in relation to folklore research and Marxism.

NAME INDEX

Non-italic Arabic numbers refer to citations. Numbers in italics indicate other than direct authorship (e.g., editor, contributor, reviewer). Italic Roman numerals refer to front matter by page.

SUBJECT INDEX